At Issue

Should Vaccinations Be Mandatory?

Other Books in the At Issue Series:

At Issue

Should Vaccinations Be Mandatory?

Noël Merino, Book Editor

GREENHAVEN PRESS
A part of Gale, Cengage Learning

GALE
CENGAGE Learning

Detroit • New York • San Francisco • New Haven, Conn • Waterville, Maine • London

GALE
CENGAGE Learning™

Christine Nasso, *Publisher*
Elizabeth Des Chenes, *Managing Editor*

© 2010 Greenhaven Press, a part of Gale, Cengage Learning.

Gale and Greenhaven Press are registered trademarks used herein under license.

For more information, contact:
Greenhaven Press
27500 Drake Rd.
Farmington Hills, MI 48331-3535
Or you can visit our Internet site at gale.cengage.com

LIBRARY OF CONGRESS CATALOGING-IN-PUBLICATION DATA

Should vaccinations be mandatory? / Noël Merino, book editor.
    p. cm. -- (At issue)
    Includes bibliographical references and index.
    ISBN 978-0-7377-4691-4 (hardcover) -- ISBN 978-0-7377-4692-1 (pbk.)
  1. Vaccination. 2. Vaccination--Public opinion. I. Merino, Noël
    RA638.S53 2010
    614.4'7--dc22
                                         2009038710

Printed in the United States of America
1 2 3 4 5 6 7 13 12 11 10 09

Contents

Introduction

Vaccination is the process by which pathogenic cells are injected into a healthy person in an attempt to cause the body to develop antibodies to a particular virus or bacterium—successful creation of antibodies is referred to as immunity to the disease caused by the particular pathogen. For many diseases, after a person has had the disease once and survived, the person usually does not acquire the disease again because the body produces antibodies to resist any subsequent infections. According to the Smithsonian Institution's National Museum of American History, human beings have known for many centuries that the body develops immunity against certain diseases after infection and people have tried to develop ways to create immunity from disease without actually contracting the disease: "Inoculation originated in India or China some time before 200 B.C."[1] Today, dozens of vaccines are used worldwide, including many that governments have made mandatory for children.

In 1796, Edward Jenner created the first vaccine to prevent smallpox by injecting a boy with cowpox. (The word 'vaccine' comes from the Latin term for cowpox, *variolae vaccinae*.) Performed in the era before hypodermic syringes, Jenner scratched the substance into the boy's arm. After syringes became available a half-century later, offering a safer way to deliver vaccinations, the development of vaccines greatly increased. In the nineteenth century, vaccines for cholera, rabies, tetanus, typhoid fever, and bubonic plague were developed.[2] In the twentieth and twenty-first centuries, several dozen vaccines were developed.

As of 2009, the U.S. Centers for Disease Control and Prevention (CDC) recommends that children receive vaccines for sixteen viruses and bacteria: Diphtheria, hepatitis A, hepatitis B, *Haemophilus influenzae*, influenza, human papillomavirus

(HPV, recommended for young girls), measles, meningococcal, mumps, pertussis (whooping cough), pneumococcal, polio, rotavirus, rubella, tetanus, and varicella (chicken pox). Because some vaccines are combined, there are twelve different vaccines to deliver immunity for these sixteen diseases, but because most require multiple injections, several dozen injections are recommended throughout childhood.[3] Several of these recommended vaccines are relatively new: The hepatitis A and varicella (chickenpox) vaccines first became available in 1995, the first rotavirus vaccine came out in 1998 (but was withdrawn in 1999 and replaced in 2006), and the HPV vaccine first became available in 2006.[4]

Whereas the U.S. federal government merely recommends certain vaccines for the general public, all fifty states have school vaccination laws. These laws, which vary from state to state, mandate that children receive certain vaccines in order to attend public school, with some exceptions. The first state law mandating vaccinations for school attendance was enacted in Massachusetts in 1855 to prevent smallpox transmission in schools. The U.S. Supreme Court upheld the right of states to enact mandatory vaccinations, under the police power of the state, in *Jacobson v. Massachusetts* (1905), and rejected a Fourteenth Amendment challenge to school vaccination laws in *Zucht v. King* (1922).[5] As of 2009, all states allow exemptions to their school vaccination laws for medical reasons, forty-eight states allow religious exemptions, and twenty permit philosophical opposition as grounds for exemption.[6]

Concern about the safety and necessity of vaccines has increased in recent years. Nationwide, less than 1 percent of school children have exemptions to mandatory school vaccinations, but in certain states and certain areas within states, the number of children with exemptions is at least one in twenty.[7] Part of the reason for increased exemption and decreased vaccination can be explained by concerns about the safety of vaccines. Actors Jenny McCarthy and Jim Carrey—

board members of the organization Generation Rescue, an international movement of scientists, physicians, and volunteers researching the causes and treatments for autism—have been very vocal in the media about their concern that vaccines put children at risk for autism.[8] On the other side of the debate, physician Paul A. Offit, author of *Autism's False Prophets*, denies any link between vaccines and autism, defending the relative safety of vaccines in relation to the dangers of the diseases that vaccines prevent.[9]

Outbreaks of measles, polio, pertussis, and rubella have been documented in areas with high rates of unvaccinated children,[10] causing concern that certain diseases believed to have been stamped out are making a comeback, which places not only the unvaccinated at risk, but also those not fully vaccinated and a certain percentage of those vaccinated who do not gain full immunity. The debate about mandatory vaccination laws continues. Disagreements about the harms and benefits of vaccinations, and disagreements about the rights of parents to make health care choices potentially at the expense of a community's health, are a few of the topics covered in the viewpoints included in *At Issue: Should Vaccinations Be Mandatory?*.

Notes

1. National Museum of American History, "History of Vaccines," Smithsonian Institution. www.americanhistory.si.edu/polio/virusvaccine/history.htm. Accessed June 16, 2009.
2. Centers for Disease Control and Prevention, *Epidemiology and Prevention of Vaccine-Preventable Diseases*, 11th ed. Washington, DC: Public Health Foundation, 2009.
3. Centers for Disease Control and Prevention, "Recommended Immunization Schedules for Persons Aged 0 Through 18 Years—United States, 2009," *Morbidity and Mortality Weekly Report*, January 2, 2009. www.cdc.gov/mmwr/preview/mmwrhtml/mm5751a5.htm?s_cid=mm5751a5_e.

4. Immunization Action Coalition, "Vaccine Information for the Public and Health Professionals," April 2009. www.vaccineinformation.org.
5. Kevin M. Malone and Alan R. Hinman, "Vaccination Mandates: The Public Health Imperative and Individual Rights," in Richard A. Goodman et al., eds., *Law in Public Health Practice*, 2nd ed. New York: Oxford University Press, 2006, pp. 262–284.
6. Johns Hopkins University Bloomberg School of Public Health, "Vaccine Exemptions," April 16, 2009. www.vaccinesafety.edu/cc-exem.htm.
7. Malone and Hinman, p. 274.
8. Generation Rescue, "About Vaccines," www.generationrescue.org/vaccines.html#. Accessed June 16, 2009.
9. Claudia Kalb, "Stomping Through a Medical Minefield," *Newsweek*, November 3, 2008.
10. Malone and Hinman, p. 274.

1

Childhood Vaccinations Are Important for Public Health

U.S. Department of Health and Human Services, Centers for Disease Control and Prevention, National Center for Immunization and Respiratory Disease

A part of the Centers for Disease Control and Prevention within the U.S. Department of Health and Human Services, the National Center for Immunization and Respiratory Diseases is focused on the prevention of disease, disability, and death through immunization and control of respiratory diseases.

Immunization using childhood vaccines has prevented hundreds of millions of cases of disease since the invention of such vaccines. Vaccines work by providing recipients with immunity to disease without the recipients actually contracting the disease. Vaccines are safe, only occasionally resulting in treatable reactions. Although current infection rates for diseases that vaccines protect against are low, those diseases would likely return as epidemics, resulting in illness and deaths, if vaccines were no longer administered. It is important that all children be vaccinated according to the current recommended vaccination schedule to protect all people from preventable disease.

Immunization has been called the most important public health intervention in history, after safe drinking water. It has saved millions of lives over the years and prevented hundreds of millions of cases of disease.

Department of Health and Human Services, Centers for Disease Control and Prevention, National Center for Immunization and Respiratory Disease, *Parents' Guide to Childhood Immunizations*. Portland, OR: U.S. Government Printing Office, 2007.

The Benefits of Vaccines

We all know that getting our children immunized can protect them from some very serious diseases.

But did you know that it can also . . .

- Protect their friends, schoolmates, and others from those same diseases? *Some children can't get certain vaccines for medical reasons, or some children are not able to respond to certain vaccines. For these children, the immunity of people around them is their only protection.*

- Protect your grandchildren, their grandchildren, and future generations from diseases? *If we stopped vaccinating, diseases that are under control would eventually come back to cause epidemics. This has happened in several countries.*

- Even help rid the world of diseases that have been crippling and killing children for centuries? *Immunization allowed us to eradicate smallpox. Today polio is nearly gone, and in the future measles and other diseases will follow.*

Vaccines have a remarkable track record. For example . . .

- Diphtheria used to be one of the most dreaded of childhood diseases, killing over 10,000 people a year in the United States. After we started vaccinating children in the 1930s and 1940s the disease began to disappear. Today most doctors will never see a single case of diphtheria, much less have a patient die from it.

- In 1962, the year before measles vaccine was introduced, almost 500,000 cases of measles were reported in the United States, and many more cases went unreported. Ten years later there were about 32,000 cases and 10 years after that fewer than 2,000. As of the end of 2005, there have been only 405 cases in this century.

- Parents in the 1950s were terrified as polio paralyzed children by the thousands. Then we learned how to prevent polio using the Salk and Sabin vaccines. There has not been a case of wild virus polio in the United States since 1979.

- Smallpox was one of the most devastating diseases the world has ever known. It killed millions of people every year. In 1967 the World Health Organization undertook an intensive, worldwide vaccination campaign. Twelve years later the disease had been wiped out, and there hasn't been a single case since. Smallpox is the first, and so far the only, disease we have ever eradicated from the Earth; and it was thanks to vaccination.

Immunity to Disease

When disease germs enter your body, they start to reproduce. Your immune system recognizes these germs as foreign invaders and responds by making proteins called antibodies. These antibodies' first job is to help destroy the germs that are making you sick. They can't act fast enough to prevent you from becoming sick, but by eliminating the attacking germs, antibodies help you to get well.

The antibodies' second job is to protect you from future infections. They remain in your bloodstream, and if the same germs ever try to infect you again—even after many years—they will come to your defense. Only now that they are experienced at fighting these particular germs, they can destroy them before they have a chance to make you sick. This is immunity. It is why most people get diseases like measles or chickenpox only once, even though they might be exposed many times during their lifetime.

This is a good system for preventing disease. The only drawback is obvious—you have to get sick before you become immune.

How Vaccines Work

Vaccines solve this problem. They help you develop immunity without getting sick first.

Children in the United States routinely get vaccines that protect them from 14 diseases.

Vaccines are made from the same germs (or parts of them) that cause disease—measles vaccine is made from measles virus, for instance, and *Haemophilus influenzae* type B (Hib) vaccine is made from parts of the Hib bacteria. But the germs in vaccines are either killed or weakened so they won't make you sick.

Vaccines containing these weakened or killed germs are introduced into your body, usually by injection. Your immune system reacts to the vaccine the same as it would if it were being invaded by the disease—by making antibodies. The antibodies destroy the vaccine germs just as they would the disease germs—like a training exercise. Then they stay in your body, giving you immunity. If you are ever exposed to the real disease, the antibodies are there to protect you.

Immunizations help your child's immune system do its work. The child develops protection against future infections, the same as if he or she had been exposed to the natural disease. Except with vaccines your child doesn't have to get sick first to get that protection.

The Purpose of Vaccines

The purpose of immunizations is to prevent disease. Today, children in the United States routinely get vaccines that protect them from 14 diseases. All of these diseases have, at one time or another, been a serious threat to children in this country. Most of them are now at their lowest levels in history, thanks to years of immunization.

Because we don't see these diseases every day they might not seem as scary as they used to. Some of them might not even be familiar to many parents. Fifty years ago, measles was one of the most common diseases in the country—virtually every child got it. But today, most parents will never know a child with measles; in fact, most doctors will never see a case.

> *Children have very robust immune systems, and can easily cope with multiple vaccines given on the same day.*

But measles still infects about 23 million people around the world every year and kills about 480,000 of them. An infected person can travel to the United States, and we can travel anywhere in the world. A single case of disease will remain a single case if everyone around the infected person is immune. If they are not, a single case can turn into an epidemic. By vaccinating we will make sure these 14 diseases will not become everyday events for our children ever again....

Vaccine Side Effects

Contrary to a fairly common misperception, children have very robust immune systems, and can easily cope with multiple vaccines given on the same day.

While vaccines are very safe, like any medicine they do sometimes cause reactions. Mostly, these are mild "local" reactions (soreness or redness where the shot is given) or a low-grade fever. They last a day or two and then go away. Sometimes more serious reactions are associated with vaccines. These are much less common. Some of them are clearly caused by the vaccine; some have been reported after vaccination but are so rare that it is impossible to tell if they were caused by the vaccine or would have happened anyway....

Some children also have allergies, and occasionally a child will have a severe allergy to a substance that is component of a vaccine. There is a very small risk (estimated at around one in a million) that a vaccine could trigger a severe reaction in a child who has such an allergy. Should one of these allergic reactions occur, it would usually happen within several minutes to several hours after the vaccination, and would be characterized by hives, difficulty breathing, paleness, weakness, hoarseness or wheezing, a rapid heart beat, and dizziness. Doctors' offices are equipped to deal with these reactions. . . .

Questions About Vaccines

Why do children need so many shots?

Some of us may have gotten only 3 vaccines as children: DTP [diphtheria, tetanus, and pertussis], polio, and smallpox. There were no vaccines for measles, chickenpox, mumps, and other diseases—which meant that many of us also got those diseases! Over the years scientists have developed vaccines against more diseases, and we give them to our children to protect them from those diseases. Children don't get smallpox vaccine any more because we have eradicated the disease. Within our lifetimes, we may also eradicate polio, and then that vaccine too will no longer be needed. More combination vaccines may also reduce the number of shots children will need. At the same time, vaccines may be developed to protect us against even more diseases.

Why are vaccines given at such an early age?

Vaccines are given at an early age because the diseases they prevent can strike at an early age. Some diseases are far more serious or common among infants or young children. For example, up to 60% of severe disease caused by *Haemophilus influenzae* type b occurs in children under 12 months of age. Of children under 6 months of age who get pertussis, 72% must be hospitalized, and 84% of all deaths from pertussis are among children less than 6 months of age. The ages at which vaccines are recommended are not arbitrary. They are chosen to give children the earliest and best protection against disease.

What if my child misses a dose of vaccine?

They can continue the series where they left off. Vaccinations do not have to be repeated when there is a longer-than-recommended interval between doses.

How safe are vaccines?

They are very safe. But like any medicine, they are not perfect. They can cause reactions. Usually these are mild, like a sore arm or slight fever. Serious reactions are very uncommon. Your health-care provider will discuss the risks with you before your child gets each vaccine, and will give you a form called a Vaccine Information Statement, which describes the vaccine's benefits and risks. The important thing to remember is that getting vaccines is much safer than getting the diseases they prevent.

Do vaccines always work?

Vaccines work most of the time, but not always. Most childhood vaccinations work between 90% and 100% of the time. Sometimes, though, a child may not respond to certain vaccines, for reasons that aren't entirely understood. This is one reason why it is important for all children to be immunized. A child who does not respond to a vaccine has to depend on the immunity of others around her for protection. If my child is immune to measles, he can't infect your child who failed to respond to measles vaccine. But if my child never got the vaccine, he can not only get measles himself, he can pass it along to others who are not immune.

Questions About Not Vaccinating

What will happen if my child doesn't get his vaccinations?

One of two things could happen:

1. If your child goes through life without ever being exposed to any of these diseases, nothing will happen.

2. If your child is exposed to one of these diseases, there is a good chance he will get it. What happens then depends on the child and the disease. Most likely he would

get ill and have to stay in bed for a few days up to 1–2 weeks. But he could also get very sick and have to go to the hospital. At the very worst, he could die. In addition, he could also spread the disease to other children or adults who are not immune.

What are my child's chances of being exposed to one of these diseases?

Even if disease rates are low now, if we stopped vaccinating they wouldn't remain low for very long.

Overall, quite low. Some of these diseases have become very rare in the United States (thanks to immunizations), so the chances of exposure are small. Others, such as varicella [chickenpox] and pertussis [whooping cough], are still relatively common. Some are rare in the U.S. but common elsewhere in the world, so there is risk not only to travelers, but also to anyone exposed to travelers from other countries visiting here.

If my child's risk of exposure to disease is so low, why should I bother getting him immunized?

This is a good question. One answer, of course, is that even if the risk of getting these diseases is low, it is not zero. If only one child in the whole country gets diphtheria this year, that child has a 1 in 10 chance of dying. Vaccination would have protected him.

But there is also another answer. Even if disease rates are low now, if we stopped vaccinating they wouldn't remain low for very long. We know this because it has already happened in several countries, including Great Britain and Japan. For instance, in 1974, about 80% of Japanese children were being vaccinated against pertussis. That year Japan had only 393 pertussis cases and no deaths. But then there was a national scare about the safety of pertussis vaccine, and over the next few years the vaccination rate dropped to about 10%. In 1979 the country suffered a major pertussis epidemic with more than 13,000 cases and 41 deaths. When routine vaccination was reinstated, disease rates dropped again. Without the protection afforded by a highly immunized population, diseases could make a comeback here too.

Vaccine Ingredients

The major ingredient of any vaccine is a killed or weakened form of the disease organism the vaccine is designed to prevent. Therefore, measles vaccine is mostly measles virus. Pneumococcal vaccine is mostly the surface coating from pneumococcal bacteria.

In addition, vaccines can contain:

- Diluents—A diluent is a liquid used to dilute a vaccine to the proper concentration. It is usually saline or sterile water.

- Adjuvants—Adjuvants are chemicals added to vaccines to make them provide stronger immunity. Various forms of aluminum salts are the most commonly used adjuvants in vaccines.

- Preservatives—Preservatives are included in some vaccines (mainly ones that come in multi-dose vials that are used more than once) to prevent bacterial growth that could contaminate the vaccine.

- Stabilizers—Some vaccines contain stabilizers (for example, gelatin or lactose-sorbitol), to keep them safe and effective under different conditions or different temperatures.

- Remnants from manufacturing—Chemicals are often used during the vaccine manufacturing process, and then removed from the final product. For example, formalin might be used to kill a vaccine virus, or antibiotics might be used to prevent bacterial contamination.

When these chemicals are removed, a tiny trace may remain. While some of these chemicals might be harmful in large doses, the trace amounts left in vaccines are too small to have a toxic effect.

2

Some Worries About Childhood Vaccinations Are Legitimate

Gary Null and Martin Feldman

Gary Null, an advocate of alternative medicine and natural healing, is the host of the radio program Natural Living with Gary Null *and coauthor of* Germs, Biological Warfare, Vaccinations: What You Need to Know. *Martin Feldman is an assistant clinical professor of neurology at Mount Sinai School of Medicine in New York City.*

There are many legitimate concerns about vaccinations. Vaccines may provoke latent illnesses and do not result in real immunity. The fact that vaccines are mandated and funded without choice is dangerous to consumers who have no freedom in the situation. Furthermore, the right to refuse vaccination varies from state to state and is not guaranteed. Individuals should have the power to gather information about vaccines and make up their own minds. Given the possible dangers associated with vaccines, strengthening the immune system in alternative ways may be preferable to subjecting the body to these substances that could cause more harm than good.

Those who take issue with universal immunization point out that the programs do not distinguish between children who may benefit from a certain vaccine and those who may be hurt by it. Infants are given blanket immunization re-

Gary Null and Martin Feldman, "Vaccination: An Updated Analysis of the Health Risks—Part 3," *Townsend Letter: The Examiner of Alternative Medicine*, issue 293, December 2007, pp. 117–20. Reproduced by permission of the authors.

gardless of their previous or current state of health and their varying susceptibilities to side effects. Ideally, the vaccination system should be much more selective, with parents being given complete information, so they can decide whether the risks associated with a particular procedure outweigh its potential benefits. Just as different races may suffer disproportionately from allergies and food sensitivities, studies indicate that they may experience different reactions to vaccines.

People engaged in the fight against government-mandated vaccines share their concerns here about several vaccination issues.

Provocation Disease

One of the most hazardous and insidious effects of vaccination lies in its potential to induce other forms of disease, a phenomenon known as provocation disease. The mechanisms that cause this to happen are unclear, although many scientists believe that latent viruses—those already existing in a person—may be stimulated by vaccinations and that this process may be enough to activate a particular illness. Vaccination, therefore, may not be the sole cause but rather the final trigger of an illness.

Autoimmune diseases such as Guillain-Barre syndrome and thrombocytopenia have been associated with vaccinations.

In his book *Vaccination and Immunization: Dangers, Delusions and Alternatives*, Leon Chaitow states that there is no way of knowing when such latent or incubating situations may be operating, and therefore no way of knowing when a vaccine may produce this sort of provocation. He warns that provocation of a latent virus is a potentially dangerous possibility with every vaccination procedure.

Many diseases thought to be caused at least partially by vaccinations do not surface until years later, by which time it is difficult to prove a connection. Two examples of conditions that may be provoked by vaccines are as follows:

- *Allergies.* According to Dr. Harris Coulter, co-author of *A Shot in the Dark*, and other experts, vaccines and allergies are clearly connected. "What does allergy mean? It means that your body is ready to react very, very quickly when exposed a second time to a substance to which it is allergic. If you are allergic to ragweed, [a small amount] of ragweed will start you sneezing. Now, if you vaccinate a person against pertussis or some other bacillus, you are making that person 'allergic' to that bacillus. That's what being vaccinated actually means. It means you are 'allergic' to that bacillus, in the sense that your body will react very, very rapidly if exposed to that bacillus a second time."

- *Immunosuppression and Autoimmune Disease.* The body needs to experience a full inflammatory response to create immunity, and vaccines do not allow this to happen. Instead, a chronic condition is created that can set the stage for autoimmune disease. Autoimmune diseases such as Guillain-Barre syndrome [paralysis] and thrombocytopenia [a serious blood disorder] have been associated with vaccinations.

In *Immunization: The Reality Behind the Myth*, author Walene James suggests that vaccinations may induce autoimmune disorders because "live viruses, the primary antigenic material of [some] vaccines, are capable of surviving or remaining latent in the host cell for years, without provoking acute disease." Live virus vaccines include those for chickenpox, measles, mumps, rubella, and oral polio.

Cynthia Cournoyer, author of *What About Immunizations?*, believes a key principle involved in the many negative effects of vaccines is that the immune system can tolerate only so many challenges, especially before it is given a chance to develop to maturity. "Every child," she writes, "is born with a finite ability to combat disease. This is his total immune capacity. Once a child experiences a particular disease, permanent immunity is extremely efficient, using probably three percent to seven percent of the total immune capacity of an individual. In the case of routine childhood vaccination, it is likely that as much as 30% to 70% of total immune capacity becomes committed."

Cournoyer proposes that this effect on immunity may substantially reduce a child's immunological reserves. "Far from producing a genuine immunity, a vaccine may actually interfere with or suppress the immune response as a whole, in much the same way that radiation, chemotherapy, and corticosteroids and other anti-inflammatory drugs do." Cournoyer continues, "Although the body will not make antibodies against its own tissues, viruses becoming part of the genetic make-up may cause cells to appear foreign to the immune system, making them a fair target for antibody production. . . . Under proper conditions, these latent pro viruses could become activated and cause a variety of diseases, including rheumatoid arthritis, multiple sclerosis, lupus erythematosus . . . and cancer."

Vaccines are the only products in the US that are legally mandated to be used by every person born.

Temporary Immunity of Vaccines

Vaccines provide only temporary immunity, whereas the contraction of an actual disease confers permanent immunity most of the time. Viera Scheibner, a retired research scientist, writes that "generations of children with this inadequate immunity would grow into adults with no placental immunity to pass on to their children, who would then contract measles at an age when babies are normally protected by maternal antibody. . . .

"Perhaps the most unfortunate thing about the idea of eliminating infectious diseases by vaccination is that indeed there is no need to do so. As pointed out by the group of Swiss doctors opposing the US-inspired policy of mass vaccination against measles, mumps, and rubella in Switzerland, 'We have lost the common sense and the wisdom that used to prevail in the approach to childhood diseases. Too often, instead of reinforcing the organism's defenses, fever and symptoms are relentlessly suppressed. This is not always without consequences . . .'"

Lastly, Scheibner states, "There is no need to artificially immunize our children and ourselves. The body has proper, natural mechanisms to create immunity to diseases. The diseases themselves are the priming and challenging mechanisms of the maturation process leading to the competence of the immune system. . . ."

Economic and Legal Issues

Cynthia Cournoyer has noted that vaccines are the only products in the US that are legally mandated to be used by every person born. Barbara Loe Fisher, cofounder and president of the National Vaccine Information Center (NVIC), Vienna, Virginia, has advocated the right of individuals to make informed, independent vaccination decisions for themselves and their children for two decades. She paints an ominous picture of things to come: "As consumers, we can bring very little economic pressure on the system to have that product improved or removed, because all of us are required by law to use it. It's a dream for the pharmaceutical industry involved in making vaccines, because there's no way anybody can say no. It's a stable, ready-made market, and the enactment of the compensation law in 1986 has removed almost all liability for drug companies. . . ."

Fisher cautions that state health departments may develop electronic systems to monitor the vaccination status of each child. "... If we don't act now, the public health infrastructure is going to get more power to intrude in our lives, intrude in our health care choices. It all comes down to whether or not we, as individuals, are going to fight for the right to make informed health care choices, including vaccination choices, for ourselves and our children, and whether we are going to hold the drug companies and government health officials accountable for the injuries, deaths, and chronic illnesses caused by the vaccines they produce, sell, and promote for mass use."

The National Childhood Vaccine Injury Act of 1986 created a no-fault compensation program through which plaintiffs can seek compensation for injuries from vaccines recommended for routine administration. The law also provided, however, that evidence of gross negligence would be needed to seek punitive damages against vaccine manufacturers. The NVIC said in 2003 that it and other parent groups "have been critical of how adversarial the system is and how difficult it is to get an award." Through fiscal year 2001, the National Vaccine Injury Compensation Program had paid $1.3 billion in total awards (petitioner's awards and attorney's fees) for approximately 1,660 compensable petitions.

All states have laws mandating the vaccination of children before they enter school, but these laws also allow for various types of exemptions to compulsory vaccination.

The compensation program is funded through an excise tax on vaccines. As a result, consumers foot the bill for any injuries or deaths that may result from medical procedures they are required by law to undergo. Alan Phillips, co-founder of Citizens for Healthcare Freedom, notes: "[Pharmaceutical companies] have been allowed to use gag orders as a leverage tool in vaccine damage legal settlements to prevent disclosure of information to the public about vaccination dangers. Such arrangements are clearly unethical; they force a non-consenting American public to pay for vaccine manufacturers' liabilities, while attempting to ensure that this same public will remain ignorant of the dangers of their products."

Vaccine critic Randall Neustaedter adds: "When lawsuits leveled at drug companies began wiping out profits gleaned from the pertussis vaccine, the manufacturers simply stopped production of the vaccine. The United States government stepped in to pay these vaccine-damage claims. Only then did the drug companies agree to resume vaccine production. . . ."

Right to Refuse Vaccination

All states have laws mandating the vaccination of children before they enter school, but these laws also allow for various types of exemptions to compulsory vaccination. Parents may seek exemptions on behalf of their children. According to the NVIC, all 50 states allow exemptions based on medical reasons, 48 states allow exemptions for people who have a sincere religious belief opposing vaccination, and 18 states allow exemptions based on philosophical, personal, or conscientiously held beliefs.

The ease of obtaining a vaccination exemption may depend on the type sought and the requirements of the individual's state. In the journal *Pediatrics*, researchers say that "in many states, it is easier to claim a religious or philosophical exemption than to adhere to mandated immunization requirements." On the other hand, Kurt Link, MD, states in *The Vaccine Controversy* that exemptions are often very difficult to obtain and that less than two percent of people who apply for a vaccination exemption obtain one. Link says that parents who are denied an exemption and try to defy the vaccination mandate may have their children excluded from school, may be charged with criminal child abuse or neglect, and may have their children taken into state custody.

Potential Downside to Exemptions

Parents who refuse vaccinations for their children should be aware of other potential consequences as well. The literature shows that unvaccinated children may be at greater risk of contracting diseases covered by routine vaccines. In the *Pediatrics* article, the authors cite research showing that "exemptors" were 22 times more likely to contract measles than were vaccinated people and six times more likely to contract pertussis. In addition, unvaccinated people account for the majority of recent cases of tetanus. A study published in 2006 also found that states allowing personal-belief exemptions and states with easier exemption processes were associated with a higher incidence of pertussis.

The point is that individuals need the freedom to choose.

Another consideration is that pediatricians may dismiss patients who refuse to be vaccinated. In a survey of 1004 members of the American Academy of Pediatrics published in 2005, 39% said they would dismiss a family for refusing all vaccinations, and 28% would dismiss a family for refusing select vaccines.

Varying State Laws

According to the NVIC, parents who want to exempt a child from mandated vaccination must know what types of exemptions the law in their state allows and the type of proof that may be required. In many states offering philosophical or personal-belief exemptions, for example, a parent must object to all vaccines, not particular ones. With medical exemptions, some states will accept without question a letter from a physician saying that one or more vaccines would be detrimental to the health of the patient, while the health departments in other states review such exemptions and may decide one is not justified. With religious exemptions, says the NVIC, state laws differ regarding the definition of the exemption and the proof needed of one's religious beliefs opposing vaccination. In fact, the NVIC does not provide or recommend a prewritten waiver for religious exemptions. If a prewritten waiver does not meet your state's requirements, you may draw attention to your child and, if challenged on the exemption, end up in litigation with your state or county health department in which you must prove your religious beliefs. . . .

Freedom to Choose

The point is that individuals need the freedom to choose. They should not be forced in one direction or another. Fisher stresses this: "Our organization does not tell a parent what to do. I want to make that clear. We are an information clearinghouse, and we believe in education. We believe that parents should take the responsibility for making their own decision. In this society, we ought to have the right to make the right decisions without being bullied and harassed and threatened into vaccinating if we do not believe that it is in the best interest of our child."

Alan Phillips adds, "I don't advocate that people do or do not vaccinate. I say that there's a lot of information that people should investigate before they make a decision one way or the other. We're so steeped in what I would now call the myth of vaccination that it seems nonsensical and counterintuitive to even raise the question. In fact, the first time that I raised the question with a pediatrician I got yelled at. While I think that was unprofessional of the pediatrician, it does demonstrate the degree to which assumptions about vaccinations are held."

Dr. Dean Black, author of *Immunizations: Compulsion or Choice*, states, "As a parent, there might be times I choose to immunize my child. Maybe I would find scientific evidence to back its validity in a case where a disease is so fraught with risk that I dare not expose my child. Maybe then I would choose [to vaccinate]. But I would do so having thoroughly thought about it. . . . What I believe we cannot tolerate as a free nation is to have government bureaucrats come in and say—based upon false statistics—if you don't immunize your child, you will suffer penalty of law. That, to me, is a gross injustice that simply has to be changed."

The Holistic Health Movement

Fisher believes that if we are concerned about our health and our freedoms, we should be worrying about the future. "I truly believe that unless the public wakes up to what is happening, and starts standing up for their right to be fully informed about vaccines and their right to make informed independent vaccine decisions, the day will come when we won't have that right. We will be forcibly vaccinated by law without exception."

We do not yet know a single silver-bullet remedy for all childhood illnesses that are known to cause no harm to the future adult.

Fisher urges everyone to stop being complacent, to start becoming informed about vaccines and diseases, and to act. Specifically, she states, "You are going to have to work to amend your state's laws. If you would like to be better informed and to help get the truth out, please join our grassroots vaccine safety movement."

Fisher believes that alternative healthcare modalities in the US will play an important role in the vaccine safety movement. "Those who are looking into . . . osteopathic medicine, naturopathic, homeopathic, vitamin therapy, etc., are looking for ways to boost the immune system through more natural means in order to be able to naturally deal with viruses and bacteria that they come in contact with. This is a very important movement."

Dr. Black agrees. He sees vaccinations as a shortcut for people in our society who have not taken full responsibility for their health. "It's a way of saying, don't look at the more natural holistic way of helping the body. Medicine believes disease is the enemy. . . . Medicine fights disease. Natural health care works with it. . . . Medicine believes symptoms are evil. Natural health care believes symptoms are the body's efforts to rid itself of disease."

Curtis Cost, author of *Vaccines Are Dangerous: A Warning to the Black Community*, adds, ". . . parents do not need to be terrified into believing that the only way to protect themselves and their children from disease is through vaccines. We know that if parents breast-feed their babies, the risk of death and disease is dramatically reduced because the breast milk contains all the natural nutrients that the mother will naturally give to her child as she breast-feeds. We know that diet has a tremendous effect on disease. If you are not eating a proper diet, your risk of getting various diseases is much greater. So we need to focus on taking control of our health . . . to focus on eating more organically grown fresh fruits and vegetables, on drinking pure water, and on exercising. These actions build up the immune system."

It stands to reason that our approach might be better directed at bolstering natural immunity, by strengthening the body's own disease-fighting capability, than trying to manipulate a carefully balanced system which may or may not tip to the detriment of the future individual. The old adage, "What doesn't kill you makes you stronger" describes the credo of the vaccine industry. The problem is that we do not yet know a single silver-bullet remedy for all childhood illnesses that are known to cause no harm to the future adult.

3

Given the Risks, Vaccinations Should Not Be Mandated

Neil Z. Miller

Neil Z. Miller is a medical research journalist, the director of the Thinktwice Global Vaccine Institute, and the author of Vaccine Safety Manual for Concerned Families and Health Practitioners.

Vaccines pose many risks and, because of this, parents should not be obligated to have their children vaccinated. The claim that unvaccinated children will put vaccinated children at risk for disease makes no sense if the vaccines work the way they are supposed to work. There are many new mandatory vaccines, such as the vaccines for hepatitis B and chicken pox, that are clearly unnecessary. The unethical behavior of members of governmental health organizations and pharmaceutical executives in recent years should make the general public suspicious about the claimed benefits of vaccines. There is no indication that public health is improved with mandatory vaccinations.

Parents should not be obligated to play Russian Roulette with their children. Vaccines pose serious risks. These hazards are acknowledged by vaccine manufacturers in their product inserts, documented in numerous studies, substantiated by the federal government's Vaccine Adverse Event Reporting System (VAERS), and confirmed anecdotally by parents. For example, the MMR [measles, mumps, and rubella] vaccine manufacturer concedes that diabetes, thrombocytopenia (a serious blood disorder), arthritis, encephalitis (brain inflammation), Guillain-Barre syndrome (paralysis), and death, have all been reported during clinical trials of its vaccine. Peer-reviewed studies link the haemophilus influenzae type b (Hib) vaccine to epidemics of type 1 diabetes, the hepatitis B vaccine to autoimmune and neurological disorders, and the flu vaccine to paralytic ailments. These are just a few examples. Medical and scientific journals contain hundreds of other peer-reviewed studies linking vaccines to debilitating ailments. In addition, every year approximately 14,000 people file vaccine adverse reaction reports with the CDC [Centers for Disease Control and Prevention]. In just the past 26 months—as of August 2008—more than 8,500 young American females filed adverse reaction reports after receiving the new HPV [human papillomavirus] vaccine. Nearly 600 of these cases were labeled "serious," requiring hospitalization, resulting in life-threatening disabilities, or death. VAERS is a passive reporting system, so the number of people believed to be hurt by vaccines is vastly underreported. According to Dr. David Kessler, former head of the FDA [Food and Drug Administration], "only about 1 percent of serious events—adverse drug reactions—are reported." This is confirmed by the Thinktwice Global Vaccine Institute, which receives unsolicited personal stories of vaccine damage every day. The families telling these dreadful stories rarely file official reports. Of course, these stories do not constitute "proof" of vaccine damage—at least no more than a child's cry after skinning his knee is "proof" of pain. However, patterns of adverse vaccine reactions are easily observed when unrelated families consistently report similar stories of healthy children prior to their shots, and hospitalized children after their shots.

These patterns tell a larger story. A medical industry that errs on the side of denial rather than concern is backward and criminally negligent. In an enlightened healthcare community, we would listen to the larger story with sincerity, and opt to protect additional children from harm. Pretending that serious reactions to vaccines are rare does not make it true, incapacitates our children, and degrades our society. Since reputed vaccine risk-to-benefit ratios are bogus, and pharmaceutical shots are considerably more unsafe than officially acknowledged, *it is morally unconscionable to mandate vaccines for entry into an educational institution.*

The Vaccinated and Unvaccinated

Unvaccinated children cannot threaten vaccinated children if the shots are effective. When students contract disease, vaccine proponents are quick to blame the outbreaks on unvaccinated children. Yet, the official data tell a different story: a majority of cases occur in fully vaccinated populations. Dr. William Atkinson, senior epidemiologist with the CDC, admitted that "measles transmission has been clearly documented among vaccinated persons. In some large outbreaks . . . over 95% of cases have a history of vaccination." Similar problems with vaccine efficacy plague other vaccines as well. For example, in a 2003 outbreak of pertussis, 4 of every 5 people who contracted the disease were vaccinated against it. In 2006, there was a large outbreak of mumps in the United States; 92% of the cases were in people who were vaccinated against mumps. Such data provides evidence that herd immunity—the idea that when a proportion of people within a targeted population are *immune* to a disease, transmission rates are reduced—may not apply to *vaccinated* populations. Vaccination and immunity are not synonymous.

Authorities claim that vaccines won't work for society unless a very high number of people in the targeted population—school children—take them. Apparently, unvaccinated children are a threat to the group. But this does not make sense. By this reasoning, the unvaccinated—who are being coerced into taking the shots—*are somehow responsible for pro-*

tecting the vaccinated. How ironic! If some students are vaccinated, that's their family's choice. If other students are unvaccinated, that's their family's informed decision as well. Vaccinated students take their chances hoping to avoid serious adverse reactions, while unvaccinated students risk contracting the disease. However, *if vaccinated students contract the disease, the shot was ineffective, NOT the fault of unvaccinated students.* Officials ignore their own ineffective vaccine, choosing instead to smear the unvaccinated. Outrage should be vented in the proper direction—at those who developed ineffective shots and falsely promoted a defective product.

Low-risk children are being force-vaccinated to protect high-risk adults or to increase the vaccine manufacturer's profits.

Unnecessary Vaccines

Some vaccines required for school entry are clearly unnecessary. Our children have become captive instruments of the vaccine industry, accessible by mandate to satisfy other purposes. For example, children rarely develop hepatitis B. In the United States, less than 1% of all reported hepatitis B cases occur in persons less than 15 years of age. When the hepatitis B vaccine was initially introduced, 87% of pediatricians did NOT believe it was needed by their patients. Doctors knew that children *rarely* develop this disease. According to the hepatitis B vaccine manufacturer, children are targeted "because a vaccination strategy limited to high-risk individuals has failed." In other words, because high-risk groups—sexually promiscuous adults and IV [intravenous] drug users—are difficult to reach or have rejected this vaccine, authorities are targeting children. Authorities believe that by vaccinating children (a low-risk *herd*) they will protect unvaccinated adults (a high-risk *herd*). Since children are unlikely to contract hepatitis B, and studies show that vaccine efficacy declines after a few years, *children are being subjected to all of the risks of the hepatitis B vaccine without the expected benefit.*

The chickenpox vaccine is another drug that should not have been mandated for all children. It was available since the 1970s but authorities were reluctant to license and promote it because the disease is rarely dangerous and confers lifelong immunity. The vaccine, however, contains a weakened form of the virus; once injected, it remains in the body indefinitely. Authorities were concerned that it could reawaken years after the vaccination and cause serious problems. In addition, the chickenpox vaccine was originally developed for children with leukemia or compromised immune systems, a small population at greater risk for complications from the disease. But vaccine manufacturers quickly sought a wider market for their potentially lucrative product. A study conducted by the CDC in 1985 determined that the vaccine was not necessary. However, in 1995 it was promoted as "cost-effective"—rather than essential—because moms and dads would not have to miss work and stay home (an average of 1 day) to care for their sick children. It was licensed shortly thereafter. *Before* the chickenpox vaccine was licensed, doctors would encourage parents to expose their children to the disease while they were young. Doctors recommended this course of action because they knew that chickenpox is relatively harmless when contracted prior to the teenage years (but more dangerous in adolescents and adults). However, *after* the vaccine was licensed, the CDC began warning parents about the dangers of chickenpox. Doctors stopped encouraging parents to expose their children to this disease. Instead, they were told to have their children vaccinated against chickenpox.

These examples confirm that some vaccines required for school entry are NOT essential. School officials have become henchmen for the vaccine industry. Low-risk children are being force-vaccinated to protect high-risk adults or to increase the vaccine manufacturer's profits. Blackmailing families by *threatening to withhold a child's education for refusing needless vaccines is a moral outrage.*

Conflicts of Interest

Conflicts of interest permeate the vaccine industry. Vaccine recommendations and other important healthcare decisions that affect our nation's children are frequently based on ulterior motives. Safety and protection are NOT always top priorities. Instead, authorities may be influenced by monetary considerations or the urge to manipulate undesirable study results. For example, in June of 2000, two separate yet highly significant events rocked the vaccine industry:

Event #1: Congress held a hearing to determine if "the entire process [of licensing and recommending vaccines] has been polluted and the public trust has been violated." Two years earlier, vaccine authorities had evidence that a new vaccine under consideration (for diarrhea!) was dangerous, yet that didn't stop them from licensing and recommending it for every child in the USA. This vaccine was linked to numerous cases of a life-threatening intestinal blockage and baby deaths. After this vaccine was withdrawn from the market, Congress discovered that 60% of the FDA advisory committee members who voted to license this defective vaccine, and 50% of the CDC advisory committee members who voted to recommend it for every child in the country, had financial ties to the drug company that produced the vaccine or to two other companies developing their own potentially lucrative competing vaccines. For example, an FDA committee member who voted to license the defective vaccine had received more than $250,000 per year in research funds from the drug company that made the vaccine. A CDC committee member who voted to recommend the defective vaccine for every child was paid by the industry to travel around the country teaching doctors that vaccines are safe. In addition, he held a potentially lucrative patent on a similar vaccine under development! Despite this important Congressional exposé, no one at the FDA, CDC, or U.S. Department of Health and Human Services admitted a problem, and claimed that it's perfectly acceptable for committee members with obvious conflicts of interest to make healthcare recommendations for every child in this country— even when they stand to benefit financially from their own decisions!

Withholding a child's education for refusing vaccines when crucial studies purporting to prove their safety are bogus, is both reprehensible and indefensible.

A Secret Conference

Event #2: Just one week prior to the Congressional investigation into conflicts of interest within the vaccine industry, a top-secret meeting of high-level officials from the CDC, FDA, World Health Organization (WHO), and representatives from every major vaccine manufacturer, was held at the secluded Simpsonwood conference center in Norcross, Georgia. They had gathered to discuss an alarming new study that *confirmed a link between thimerosal (mercury) in childhood vaccines and neurological damage*, including recent dramatic increases in autistic spectrum disorders. According to the lead researcher, "We have found statistically significant relationships between the exposures and outcomes." Since 1991, when the CDC and FDA started requiring babies to receive multiple doses of thimerosal-laced hepatitis B, Hib, and the already mandated diphtheria, tetanus and pertussis shots (via [the vaccines] DPT and DTaP), cases of autism skyrocketed. Dr. Robert Chen, head of vaccine safety for the CDC, congratulated the group for their apparent success thus far at being able to keep the incriminating data out of "less responsible hands." Dr. John Clements, WHO vaccine advisor, was more blunt, declaring that perhaps the CDC study "should not have been done at all." Instead of warning the public and recalling the dangerous vaccines, this small group of federal health officials and vaccine industry executives spent the weekend calculating how to cover up the truth—and followed through on their plot over the next few years. First, the CDC's vast database on childhood vaccines was removed from public access so that unbiased researchers could not confirm the study results. Next, the incriminating data from the original study was reworked, and the new version was published in a peer-reviewed journal. However, this time "no consistent significant associations were found between thimerosal-containing vaccines and neurodevelopmental outcomes." Finally, to complete the deception, the CDC would need additional "proof" that thimerosal-laced vaccines are safe. According to Dr. Gordon Douglas, the director of strategic planning at the National Institutes of Health (and former president of vaccinations for Merck, a major vaccine manufacturer), four new studies were currently taking place *"to rule out the proposed link between autism and thimerosal."*

These two events—the Congressional hearing on conflicts of interest within the vaccine licensing and recommendation process, and the secret Simpsonwood conference—confirm that U.S. health authorities have lost their ethical bearings and have NOT made our children's safety a top priority. Requiring vaccines for school entry when they may have been added to the childhood immunization schedule simply to line the pockets of powerful authorities is dangerous and corrupt. Withholding a child's education for refusing vaccines when crucial studies purporting to prove their safety are bogus, is both reprehensible and indefensible. Thus, *every family must remain free to accept or reject vaccines.*

Vaccines Are Not Improving Health

Recovery from natural disease provides advantages over artificial immunity. Measles, mumps, rubella and chickenpox usually confer permanent immunity; the child will rarely contract these ailments again. In contrast, vaccines provide temporary immunity; protection is incomplete, requiring booster doses. Vaccinated children are still susceptible to the disease. Studies also indicate that childhood diseases can have a favorable effect on the child's immune system. When children overcome illnesses on their own, their immune systems are stimulated: they build resistance to other diseases in later life. For example, several studies show that women are less likely to develop ovarian cancer if they have had mumps in childhood.

Other countries recommend fewer vaccines and do not require them for school entry.

Few people utilize exemptions. In 1991, the CDC concluded that outbreaks of disease can be avoided if 70% to 80% of children are vaccinated. A 1992 study published in the *Journal of the American Medical Association* confirmed that vaccination rates of "80% or less" should be sufficient to protect against disease outbreaks. Most parents obediently follow their doctor's orders and vaccinate their children. In addition, schools rarely publicize legal exemptions to "mandatory" vaccines. Thus, *only about 2% of families file waivers to recommended shots.* This number could substantially increase without threatening herd immunity.

Australia doesn't mandate shots and is not overtaken by disease. In the United States, healthcare authorities, pediatricians, and school officials use coercive tactics to increase vaccination rates. Parents are intimidated and their children threatened with removal from school if vaccines are not "up to date." Other countries recommend fewer vaccines and do not require them for school entry. For example, in Australia medical intervention is not compulsory, free will is honored, yet epidemics do not occur. In fact, disease case and fatality rates are lower in many countries than in the United States. Many Americans would be shocked to learn that the U.S. has the greatest number of mandatory vaccines yet the 42nd worst infant mortality rate in the world. *Outbreaks of common ailments are manageable without requiring vaccines for school entry.*

4

Vaccine Risks Are Outweighed by the Risks of Not Vaccinating

Paul A. Offit and Louis M. Bell

Paul A. Offit is a professor of pediatrics at the University of Pennsylvania Medical School and author of Vaccinated: One Man's Quest to Defeat the World's Deadliest Diseases *and* Autism's False Prophets: Bad Science, Risky Medicine, and the Search for a Cure. *Louis M. Bell is chief of general pediatrics at the Children's Hospital of Philadelphia and coauthor with Offit of* Vaccines: What You Should Know.

Many people concerned about vaccines spread disinformation about the need for childhood vaccination. Vaccines work very well to prevent disease and are necessary, even though the diseases they prevent are not common—in fact, vaccines are part of the reason this is so. Vaccines are not entirely harmless, but the small risks are outweighed by the benefits of disease prevention. Despite claims by critics, babies can tolerate the a high number of vaccines, and these vaccines prevent diseases that can occur in infancy. Studies have disputed claims by critics that autism is caused by a particular vaccine.

It seems that almost every month newspaper articles and television programs depict the horrors of vaccines. The villains of these stories are greedy vaccine manufacturers, disin-

Paul A. Offit, From Chapter 15, "Common Concerns About Vaccines", in *Vaccines: What You Should Know*, Hoboken, NJ: John Wiley & Sons, Inc., 2003. Third Edition. Copyright © 2003 by Paul A. Offit, M.D. and Louis M. Bell, M.D. All rights reserved. Reproduced by permission of the author.

terested doctors, and burdensome regulatory agencies. The focus of the stories is that children are hurt unnecessarily by vaccines, and the tone is one of intrigue and cover-up.

Perhaps the most dangerous part of these stories (apart from the fact that they may cause many children to miss the vaccines they need) is that the explanations are presented in a manner that seems believable. Below we have listed the most commonly aired stories about vaccines and have tried to separate fact from myth.

The Myth That Vaccines Do Not Work

Probably the best example of the impact of vaccines is the vaccine that prevents meningitis caused by the bacterium *Haemophilus influenzae* type b (Hib).

Vaccines not only work, but they work phenomenally well.

The current Hib vaccine was first introduced to this country in 1990. At that time Hib was the most common cause of bacterial meningitis, accounting for approximately 15,000 cases and 400 to 500 deaths every year. The incidence of cases and deaths per year had been steady for decades. After the current Hib vaccine was introduced, the incidence of Hib meningitis declined to fewer than fifty cases per year! The power of the Hib vaccine is that most pediatricians and family practitioners working today saw its impact.

The story of the Hib vaccine is typical of all widely used vaccines. A dramatic reduction in the incidence of diseases such as measles, mumps, German measles [rubella], polio, diphtheria, tetanus, and pertussis [whooping cough] occurred within several years of the introduction of vaccines against them.

Vaccines not only work, but they work phenomenally well.

The Myth That Vaccines Are Not Necessary

In some ways, vaccines are victims of their own success. Most young parents today have never seen a case of measles, mumps, German measles, polio, diphtheria, tetanus, or whooping cough. As a result, some of these parents question the continued need for vaccines.

Vaccines should be given for three reasons:

- Some diseases are so prevalent in this country that a decision not to give a vaccine is a decision to risk that disease (for example, pertussis).

- Some diseases are still present in the environment. These diseases continue to occur, but at fairly low levels (for example, measles, mumps, and German measles). If immunization rates drop, outbreaks of these diseases will again occur and children will die from our lack of vigilance. This is exactly what happened in the late 1980s and early 1990s when immunization rates against measles dropped. The result was 11,000 hospitalizations and more than a hundred deaths caused by measles. Now, due to an increase in measles immunization rates, there are only about a hundred cases of measles and no deaths every year in the United States.

- Some diseases have been virtually eliminated from this country (such as polio and diphtheria). However, these diseases continue to cause outbreaks in other areas of the world. Given the high rate of international travel, these diseases could be easily imported by travelers or immigrants.

The Myth That Vaccines Are Not Safe

What does the word safe mean? The first definition of the word safe is "harmless." This definition would imply that any negative consequences of vaccines would make the vaccine unsafe.

Using this definition, no vaccine is 100 percent safe. Almost all vaccines can cause pain, redness, or tenderness at the site of injection. And some vaccines cause more severe side effects. For example, the pertussis (or whooping cough) vaccine can be a very rare cause of persistent, inconsolable crying or high fever. Although none of these severe symptoms results in permanent damage, they can be quite frightening to parents.

But, in truth, few things meet the definition of "harmless." Even everyday activities contain hidden dangers. For example, each year in the United States, 350 people are killed in bath- or shower-related accidents, 200 people are killed when food lodges in their windpipe, and 100 people are struck and killed by lightning. However, few of us consider eating solid food, taking a bath, or walking outside on a rainy day as unsafe activities. We just figure that the benefits of the activity clearly outweigh its risks.

The second definition of the word *safe* is "having been preserved from a real danger." This definition implies that vaccines provide safety. Using this definition, the danger (the disease) must be significantly greater than the means of protecting against the danger (the vaccine). Or, said another way, a vaccine's benefits must clearly and definitively outweigh its risks. . . .

It is very important for infants to be fully immunized against certain diseases by the time they are six months old.

The Myth That Infants Are Too Young to Get Vaccinated

Children are immunized in the first few months of life because several vaccine-preventable diseases infect them when they are very young. For example:

- Pertussis infects about 8,000 children, causing five to ten deaths every year in the United States. Almost all of the cases are in children *less than one year of age*.

- Children *under two years old* are 500 times more likely to catch Hib meningitis if someone with a Hib infection is living in the home.

- About 90 percent of *newborns* whose mothers are infected with hepatitis B will contract hepatitis and go on to develop chronic liver disease, cirrhosis, and possibly liver cancer.

For these reasons, it is very important for infants to be fully immunized against certain diseases by the time they are six months old.

Fortunately, young infants are surprisingly good at building immunity to viruses and bacteria. About 95 percent of children given DTaP, Hib, and hepatitis B virus vaccines will be fully protected by two years of age.

The Myth That It Is Better to Be Naturally Infected

It is true that "natural" infection almost always causes better immunity than vaccination (only the Hib, pneumococcal, and tetanus vaccines are better at inducing immunity than natural infection). Whereas natural infection causes immunity after just one infection, vaccines usually create immunity only after several doses are given over a number of years. For example, DTaP [diphtheria, tetanus, and pertussis], hepatitis B, and IPV [inactivated polio vaccine] are each given at least three times.

However, the difference between vaccination and natural infection is the price paid for immunity. The price paid for vaccination is the inconvenience of several shots and the occasional sore arm. The price paid for a single natural infection is usually considerably greater: paralysis from natural polio infection, mental retardation from natural Hib infection, liver failure from natural hepatitis B virus infection, deafness from natural mumps infection, or pneumonia from natural varicella [chicken pox] infection are high prices to pay for immunity.

Vaccines given in the first two years of life are literally a raindrop in the ocean of what infants' immune systems successfully encounter in their environment every day.

The Myth That Children Get Too Many Shots

Infants and young children commonly encounter and manage many challenges to their immune systems at the same time. Twenty years ago, seven vaccines were routinely recommended, and children received five shots by two years of age and as many as two shots at one time. Now that we have eleven routinely recommended vaccines, children could receive as many as twenty shots by two years of age and five shots at a single visit. Many parents are concerned about whether children can handle all these vaccines.

But vaccines are just a small part of what babies encounter every day. Although the mother's womb is free from bacteria and viruses, newborns immediately face a host of different challenges to their immune system. For example, from the minute they are born, thousands of different bacteria start to live on the skin as well as the lining of the nose, throat, and intestines. By quickly making an immune response to these bacteria, babies keep the bacteria from invading their bloodstream and causing serious disease.

In fact, babies are capable of responding to millions of different viruses and bacteria because they have billions of immunologic cells circulating in their bodies. Therefore the vaccines given in the first two years of life are literally a raindrop in the ocean of what infants' immune systems successfully encounter in their environment every day.

It is interesting to note that although children receive more vaccines today than they did a hundred years ago, when only the smallpox vaccine was routinely recommended in infancy, the number of separate immunologic challenges contained in vaccines has actually decreased! The smallpox vaccine contained about 200 viral proteins. If you add up today's eleven routinely recommended vaccines, the number of vaccine proteins and polysaccharides (complex sugars) is less than 130: diphtheria (1), tetanus (1), pertussis (2-5), polio (15), measles (10), mumps (9), rubella (5), Hib (2), varicella (69), conjugate pneumococcus (8), and hepatitis B (1). . . .

The Myth That Vaccines Cause Autism

Recently, stories carried by the media have caused some parents to fear that the combination measles-mumps-rubella (MMR) vaccine causes autism. Summarized below are (1) studies used to support the notion that MMR causes autism, (2) studies that disprove the notion that MMR causes autism, and (3) other investigations into the causes of autism.

Two studies have been cited by those claiming that the MMR vaccine causes autism. Both studies are critically flawed.

In 1998, Andrew Wakefield and colleagues published a paper in the journal *Lancet*. Wakefield's hypothesis was that the MMR vaccine caused a series of events that include intestinal inflammation, entrance into the bloodstream of proteins harmful to the brain, and consequent development of autism. In support of his hypothesis, Dr. Wakefield described twelve children with developmental delay, of whom eight had autism. All of these children had intestinal complaints and developed autism within one month of receiving MMR.

The Wakefield paper published in 1998 is flawed for two reasons: (1) About 90 percent of children in England received MMR at the time this paper was written. Because MMR is administered at a time when many children are diagnosed with autism, it would be expected that most children with autism would have received an MMR vaccine, and that many would have received the vaccine recently. The observation that some children with autism recently received MMR is, therefore, expected. However, determination of whether MMR causes autism is best made by studying the incidence of autism in *both* vaccinated and unvaccinated children. This wasn't done. (2) Although the authors claim that autism is a consequence of intestinal inflammation, intestinal symptoms were observed *after*, not before, symptoms of autism in all eight cases.

In 2002, Wakefield and coworkers published a second paper examining the relationship between measles virus and autism. The authors tested intestinal biopsy samples for the presence of measles virus from children with and without autism. Of children with autism, 75 of 91 were found to have measles virus in intestinal biopsy tissue as compared with only five of 70 patients who didn't have autism.

Four studies have been performed that disprove the notion that MMR causes autism.

On its surface, this is a concerning result. However, the second Wakefield paper is also critically flawed for the following reasons: (1) Measles vaccine virus is live and attenuated. After inoculation, the vaccine virus probably replicates (or reproduces itself) about fifteen to twenty times. It is likely that measles vaccine virus is taken up by specific cells responsible for virus uptake and presentation to the immune system (termed antigen-presenting cells, or APCs). Because all APCs are mobile, and can travel throughout the body (including the intestine), it is plausible that a child immunized with MMR would have measles virus detected in intestinal tissues using a very sensitive assay. To determine whether MMR is associated with autism, one must determine whether the finding is *spe-*

cific for children with autism. Therefore, children with or without autism must be identical in two ways. First, children with or without autism must be matched for immunization status (that is, receipt of the MMR vaccine). Second, children must be matched for the length of time between receipt of MMR vaccine and collection of biopsy specimens. Although this information was clearly available to the investigators and critical to their hypothesis, it was omitted from the paper. (2) Because natural measles virus is still circulating in England, it would have been important to determine whether the measles virus detected in these samples was natural measles virus or vaccine virus. Although methods are available to distinguish these two types of virus, the authors did not use them. (3) The method used to detect measles virus in these studies was very sensitive. Laboratories that work with natural measles virus (such as the lab where these studies were performed) are at high risk of getting results that are incorrectly positive. No mention is made in the paper as to how this problem was avoided. (4) As is true for all laboratory studies, the person who is performing the test should not know whether the sample is obtained from a case with autism or without autism (blinding). No statements were made in the methods section to assure that blinding occurred.

Studies Show the MMR Vaccine Does Not Cause Autism

Four studies have been performed that disprove the notion that MMR causes autism.

In 1999, Brent Taylor and coworkers examined the relationship between receipt of MMR and development of autism in a well-controlled study. Taylor examined the records of 498 children with autism or autism-like disorder. Cases were identified by registers from the North Thames region of England before and after the MMR vaccine was introduced into the United Kingdom in 1988. Taylor then examined the incidence and age at diagnosis of autism in vaccinated and unvaccinated children. He found that (1) the percentage of children vaccinated was the same in children with autism as in other children in the North Thames region; (2) no difference in the age of diagnosis of autism was found in vaccinated and unvaccinated children; and (3) the onset of symptoms of autism did not occur within two, four, or six months of receiving the MMR vaccine.

Subsequent studies by Natalie Smith published in the *Journal of the American Medical Association* and by Hershel Jick in the *British Medical Journal* found that the increase in the number of children reported to have autism was not associated with an increase in the use of the MMR vaccine.

The largest study to examine the relationship between the MMR vaccine and autism was reported in the *New England Journal of Medicine* in November 2002. About 537,000 children in Denmark who either did or did not receive the MMR vaccine were examined for about six years. The incidence of autism was the same in children who did or did not receive the MMR vaccine.

Very subtle symptoms of autism are present in early infancy and argues strongly against vaccines as a cause of autism.

Studies on the Causes of Autism

One of the best ways to determine whether a particular disease or syndrome is genetic is to examine the incidence in identical and fraternal twins. Using a strict definition of autism, when one twin has autism, approximately 60 percent of identical and 0 percent of fraternal twins have autism. Using a broader definition of autism (that is, autistic spectrum disorder), approximately 92 percent of identical and 10 percent of fraternal twins have autism. Therefore, autism clearly has a genetic basis.

Clues to the causes of autism can be found in studies examining when the symptoms of autism are first evident. Perhaps the best data examining when symptoms of autism are first evident are the "home-movie studies." These studies took advantage of the fact that many parents take movies of their children during their first birthday (before they have received the MMR vaccine). Home movies of children who were eventually diagnosed with autism and those who were not diagnosed with autism were coded and shown to developmental specialists. Investigators were, with a very high degree of accuracy, able to separate autistic from nonautistic children at one year of age. These studies found that subtle symptoms of autism were present earlier than some parents had suspected, and that receipt of the MMR vaccine did not precede the first symptoms of autism.

Other investigators extended the home-movie studies of one-year-old children to include videotapes of children taken at two to three months of age. Using a sophisticated movement analysis, videos from children eventually diagnosed with autism or not diagnosed with autism were coded and evaluated for their capacity to predict autism. Children who were eventually diagnosed with autism were predicted from movies taken in early infancy. This study supported the hypothesis that very subtle symptoms of autism are present in early infancy and argues strongly against vaccines as a cause of autism.

5

Mandatory Vaccinations Deny Parents Their Rights

Shana Kluck

Shana Kluck is assistant editor at United Liberty, a Web site offering news and commentary from a libertarian perspective.

Many parents have concerns about the safety of childhood vaccines. Many doctors dismiss their concerns without fully answering questions parents have. Parents should be allowed to do their own research and determine whether or not they think vaccinations are appropriate for their children. The mandatory vaccination requirements for attendance at public school deny parents their rights to raise their children as they see fit. Allowing government to override the rights of parents is dangerous and could lead to other intrusions.

Recently, New Jersey angered parents by requiring children between 6 months and 5 years that attend day care or preschool to receive a flu shot. The reasons given for laws like this are that it's in the public's best interest—supposedly, fewer children will get sick and/or die if they're all inoculated. Disease also costs companies and the state money in missed productivity and health care costs. So, what's to object to? Won't the majority benefit if everyone is vaccinated?

Safety Concerns

For most of us, yearly shots at the doctor's office were a way of life and few people gave any potential dangers a second thought. When my oldest child Molly was born 11 1/2 years ago, it didn't occur to me to question the safety and necessity of vaccines—at that point I was under the delusion that doctors always know best. I've since learned that medical professionals, who are certainly wonderful, invaluable people who make our world a better place to live in, are also fallible and, quite often, misinformed.

At Molly's one year checkup she was given the varicella vaccine, to ensure she would never get Chicken Pox, or at least limit it to a mild case if she ever did. Six months later, when we went back for her 18 month checkup, a flustered nurse asked me if Molly had received the varicella vaccine yet. Since most shots are given on an age-based schedule, I was surprised she had to ask and said as much. She told me that some 1 year olds had not received the vaccine because it had been taken off the market for a few months because of safety concerns. They were playing catch up now to make sure the children who had turned 1 during that time got the shot at their next check up.

I asked what I thought was an obvious question, "How do you know that it's safe now? And was the shot my daughter got safe?" She assured me in vague terms that it was completely safe and I had nothing to worry about. Fortunately, Molly has never suffered any ill effects from that shot (nor has she gotten the Chicken Pox), but that event was what inspired me to do a little more research into what I thought was a normal part of American childhood. What I found surprised me.

Unanswered Questions

Not long afterward I met my friend, Carol, whose teenage son had never progressed mentally beyond 6 months, and had to live in a home offering constant medical attention. Though unable to provide absolute proof, her story made it pretty clear that his problems stemmed from the DPT (diphtheria, pertussis, tetanus) shot, and subsequent booster shots, he had received as an infant. The doctors, of course, had denied all responsibility or blame, but could offer no other explanation as to why her son went from a healthy child to a near vegetable.

The more I learned about vaccines, the more I began to mistrust most of them and to question why we were giving healthy babies shots that were full of poison (mercury).

Having just had my 2nd child, I went to my pediatrician and started asking questions. Were these vaccines safe? How many children suffered from severe side effects? Were there any signs that showed genetic predisposition to reacting negatively? If doctors really believed they were safe, why was I required to always sign a form releasing the doctor from culpability should there be a negative effect? He patiently listened, but could offer no evidence—only platitudes and vague "facts".

Now, I'm not suggesting that all vaccines are dangerous, or that all parents should reject them. I do suggest some research, especially into family history to see if there have been instances of bad reactions.

Mistrust of the Pressure to Vaccinate

I continued my research and the more I learned about vaccines, the more I began to mistrust most of them and to question why we were giving healthy babies shots that were full of poison (mercury). When another friend became concerned that her 2 year old, who had received more than his share of vaccine shots because of a removed spleen, had autism, I turned my direction that way and began to find that many parents and scientists had found links between the ingredients in vaccines and autism. And who denied this the most vehemently? The ones who benefited financially from the marketing of shots—the pharmaceutical companies who manufactured them. Meanwhile, record numbers of children are being diagnosed as being on the autistic spectrum.

Though it was a battle with my pediatrician and his nurse at times, I began to delay or avoid altogether certain vaccines with my two existing children and the two more who were born later. Since I homeschool, I didn't have to worry about meeting the requirements set by public schools for attendance, but I knew that other parents who objected to vaccines for conscientious or religious reasons didn't have it quite so easy.

I also began to hear stories from other like-minded parents about the pressure they were put under by their doctors to have their children vaccinated. Or implied threats from the nurses that Child Protective Services don't look kindly upon parents who refuse vaccinations and their obligation to report parents who "put their children's health in jeopardy." In fear, some of these parents stopped taking their children to the doctor altogether, fearing their children would be removed from their home for refusing to subject their children to something they honestly believed was potentially dangerous.

How far are we, as Americans, as parents, willing to allow the federal or state governments to intrude into our homes?

Government Intrusion Threatens Freedom

Thankfully, so far, I haven't been required by the state to inoculate my children according to their time-table, but I question how long I will enjoy that freedom. In 2007, Texas Governor Rick Perry signed a law requiring young girls to receive Gardisol, a vaccine that claims to prevent cervical cancer. The outcry by parents was instant and overwhelming, especially when it became clear that Gov. Perry had benefited financially from Merck, manufacturer of Gardisol.

Simply put, does the government have the right to require parents to inoculate their children? Especially if the parents have religious, moral, or just plain common-sense objections to it? Where does this government authority stop? Can they also require us to feed our children according to a certain menu and schedule? After all, far more children suffer from obesity in America than Polio, Chicken Pox, Measles, Mumps or Rubella. How much is obesity costing America in health care expenditures and missed productivity?

How far are we, as Americans, as parents, willing to allow the federal or state governments to intrude into our homes? Where do we draw the line? At a federal level, that answer is easy—the Constitution is our standard. The real battle is at a state level, at least for now. Once federal healthcare is passed by the [Barack] Obama Administration, [Washington,] DC [lawmakers] may well feel they have the right to dictate what we eat or drink, if we exercise and other health-related issues. Though, my personal opinion is that Washington would prefer a lazy, obese population. They're much easier to control.

6

Mandatory Vaccinations Reduce the Risk of Disease for Everyone

Frances Childs

Frances Childs is a teacher at a comprehensive school in southern England.

Some parents in Great Britain are not vaccinating their children based on an unfounded fear about a particular vaccine. These parents are putting their own children and other children, particularly those who have not completed all vaccinations, at risk. Diseases such as measles are very dangerous, a fact that parents who do not vaccinate appear not to appreciate. Besides putting their children and others at risk, these parents also are alienating their own children, because many parents who do vaccinate choose to keep their own children away from unvaccinated kids.

Sipping a sludgy-looking concoction of herbs and mashed mung beans, Joanne offers me a beige lump which I have no trouble declining. It's an organic biscuit [cookie] from [the Caribbean island of] Guadeloupe, she tells me.

Chewing on her biscuit, she shakes her head. 'I don't understand it,' she says. 'Hardly anyone can come to Silas's birthday party next month.'

Unwise Parents

For a moment, I almost feel sorry for her. With ruthless efficiency, Joanne is being shoved out of our social circle.

Looking at three-year-old Silas playing on his own with his bricks, I'm tempted to tell her why. I could spell it out for her why he did not get an invitation to George's bouncy castle bash last weekend and won't be asked to come on the swimming trip that several mums are organising next week.

But in the end I simply make my excuses and leave. My three-year-old daughter Nancy won't be going to Silas's party either.

In fact, I'd come round to drop off his present because we aren't going to be seeing any more of Silas and Joanne.

They are not the only families we are cutting out of our lives. There won't be any more coffee mornings with Megan and her son Toby. We won't be going on play dates with Esther and her daughter Mimi either.

The continued refusal of parents to vaccinate is nothing short of criminal.

Quite simply, I don't want Nancy to have contact with Silas, Mimi and Toby because they haven't had the MMR jab [vaccination], which protects against measles, mumps and rubella.

Nancy has had her jab, but she won't be fully protected until she has a booster just before going to school.

The parents of Silas, Mimi and Toby are middle class and university educated, but they are behaving like morons and turning their children into pariahs.

The Danger of Measles

Until recently, measles had been eradicated in this country. But ten years ago, following research—now debunked—which appeared to link the MMR vaccine to autism, parents stopped vaccinating their children.

At first, this reaction was understandable. The autism theory was genuinely disturbing and the reaction of the medical establishment was so complacently dismissive that many reasonable people suspected a cover-up.

It didn't help matters when Prime Minister Tony Blair refused to confirm if his youngest son had been given the MMR jab.

Now, though, with eminent professors and medical research journals lining up to offer full and detailed evidence rebutting any link to autism, the continued refusal of parents to vaccinate is nothing short of criminal.

Measles is a serious illness which can lead to pneumonia and encephalitis [brain inflammation]. [In 2008], there were 1,348 confirmed cases in England and Wales. In the past couple of years, two children have died of it.

When I asked Joanne why she hadn't had Silas vaccinated, she looked shocked. 'I don't trust the doctors. I'm conducting my own research,' she said.

This consists of Googling herbalists and having webchats with like-minded mums.

Their alternative to vaccinating their children, she told me, is to give each other tips on concocting potions which they insist will ward off vicious childhood illnesses.

Middle-class twits like Joanne pottering around the kitchen brewing up potions would be amusing if it weren't so serious.

Let's remind ourselves of how things were when measles was rife. In March 1922, 80 children died in a single week.

I wonder what their parents would have said to women like Joanne, who are turning their backs on vaccination and relying on quacks peddling magic pills.

If contracted by a pregnant woman, measles can have devastating consequences.

Miscarriage, stillbirth, severe heart defects and deafness in the unborn child are all linked to measles.

Thirty-five years ago, my friend Angie Wright's dreams of motherhood turned to tragedy when she caught measles while visiting the doctor's surgery to have her pregnancy confirmed.

'The doctor told me to have an abortion. He said the disability would be so severe that it was the only option. I have regretted it ever since. I'm still grieving for my lost baby,' she says.

As the number of children who have not been immunised increases, so, too, does the likelihood of measles spreading.

Nurseries Should Refuse Unvaccinated Kids

MMR is 90 per cent effective. A booster before children begin school makes it almost 100 per cent effective.

But as more parents choose not to vaccinate their children, pre-school youngsters who have had MMR are at risk.

As the number of children who have not been immunised increases, so, too, does the likelihood of measles spreading.

'Recently, I got a letter from my daughter's nursery advising us all to get the MMR booster immediately,' says my friend Karen. Her three-year-old daughter had come into contact with not one but two children who hadn't been immunised and were possibly infected with measles.

'I was furious that other parents had been so selfish that they put other children at risk,' she says.

Karen believes nurseries should refuse to enroll children who haven't been vaccinated.

'Why should all our children be at risk because a few middle-class idiots have conspiracy theories against the medical establishment?'

In California, there is a law barring unvaccinated children from attending nursery and school. Parents face prosecution and even jail.

Now in Britain there is a growing backlash against women like Maria, who insists that spinach will protect her three-year-old son Marcus against measles.

'Vaccines are full of poisons. I can build up his immune system by ensuring he eats healthily,' she says.

In the past, she was indulged by the mums in our toddler group as slightly eccentric.

Now, though, following reports of children with measles at birthday parties mixing with pregnant women, she is being cold-shouldered by the other mothers who are appalled at the risks she is taking with all our children's health.

As I leave Joanne's house, Silas runs up to me. 'When is Nancy coming to play?' he asks.

He doesn't know that she's leaping about with several of his friends in Auntie Lou's house ten minutes' walk away.

He hasn't been invited because, as Lou said: 'I just don't want to take the risk.' I smile at him. 'Soon,' I lie. I wave and walk away.

7

Mandatory Vaccinations Threaten Religious Freedom

Mathew D. Staver

Mathew D. Staver is founder and chairman of Liberty Counsel, a nonprofit litigation, education, and policy organization dedicated to advancing religious freedom. He also is dean and a professor at Liberty University School of Law and director of the Liberty Center for Law and Policy. He is the author of Eternal Vigilance: Knowing and Protecting Your Religious Freedom.

Many people object to mandatory vaccinations for religious reasons. One reason people oppose certain vaccines is because some vaccines are made from aborted fetal tissue. People who hold religious beliefs against abortion oppose these vaccines for the same reasons they oppose abortion. Other people have deeply held religious beliefs against vaccinating in general. Unvaccinated children must not be prevented from attending school because of mandatory vaccination laws—such laws violate the right to religious freedom.

Most people associate vaccinations with the eradication of disease. Vaccinations have been a part of American life for decades. However, many people object to mandatory vaccinations for religious reasons. Oftentimes, these individuals are told that they have no choice and must receive the vaccinations or have their children vaccinated.

Derived from Aborted Fetal Tissue

You may be surprised to learn that some vaccinations are derived from aborted fetal tissue. Vaccines for chicken pox, Hepatitis-A, and Rubella, which are produced solely from aborted fetal tissue, do not have alternative, ethical versions. Even most physicians who oppose abortion do not realize that these three vaccines are made from aborted fetal tissue. The wife of one of our Liberty Counsel attorneys confronted her family doctor who wanted to inject her son with the chicken pox vaccine. When she told her doctor, who is Catholic, that the chicken pox vaccine contains aborted fetal tissue, he was surprised. The doctor was even more surprised when he skimmed through his medical book and found that she was right. He then proclaimed that he was faced with a dilemma which he must now confront.

In St. Louis County, Missouri, a county law required food handlers to obtain the Hepatitis-A vaccine as a prerequisite for employment. Several prominent Catholic newspapers published articles on the morality of using the vaccine and pointed out that the vaccine was derived from aborted fetal tissue. After the information became public, more and more physicians and parents have become deeply troubled by the ethical issues involved in the Hepatitis-A vaccine.

During the Rubella epidemic of 1964, some doctors advised pregnant women who were exposed to the disease to abort their children. The resulting virus strain became known in the science world as RA/27/3. R stands for Rubella, A stands for Abortus, 27 stands for the 27th fetus tested, and 3 stands for the 3rd tissue explant. In other words, there were 26 abortions prior to finding the right "species" with the active virus. The Rubella vaccine was then cultivated from the 27th aborted baby on the lung tissue of yet another aborted infant, WI-38. WI-38 (Wistar Institute 38) was taken from the lung tissue of an aborted baby at 3 months gestation in the 1960s. A second human cell line known as MRC-5 was derived from a male at

14 weeks gestation in the 1970s. These two aborted cell lines have been used to provide an ongoing source for many widely used vaccines, including Hepatitis-A and chicken pox.

Concerns About Adverse Vaccine Reactions

The chicken pox vaccine is known as Varivax. This vaccine was also developed with the use of aborted fetuses. It uses the human cell lines known as WI-38 and MRC-5. The chicken pox vaccine also contains MSG (monosodium glutamate). According to the Food and Drug Administration [FDA], MSG is not advised for use in infants, children, pregnant women or women of child-bearing age, and people with affective (mental/emotional) disorders. Dr. Arthur Lavin of the Department of Pediatrics at St. Luke's Medical Center in Cleveland, Ohio, strongly opposes the chicken pox vaccine.

Injecting their children with Hepatitis-B is like the state forcing the parents to give their children clean needles or condoms.

Studies show that up to 3% of chicken pox vaccine recipients actually contract chicken pox from the vaccine, and some chicken pox cases may be contracted from recently vaccinated children. Some studies suggest that chicken pox in a vaccinated child may be milder than in an unvaccinated child. However, some experts also believe that this may be due to the vaccine suppressing the illness, which can actually signal a more serious underlying chronic condition. "Atypical measles" is a disease that occurs only in people previously vaccinated for measles, and it is far more serious than regular measles. It is yet unknown if "atypical chicken pox" cases will appear as a result of the use of Varivax.

The FDA has stated that there are fewer than 10% of serious adverse reactions and deaths following vaccinations. The federal government actually pays families of vaccine-killed or

-disabled children nearly $100 million dollars each year and has done so since 1986, through the National Vaccine Injury Compensation Program.

Alternative Vaccines

There are other vaccines that are derived from aborted fetuses for which there are alternatives. For example, there are two alternatives for Hepatitis-B, Engerix and Comvax, both of which are produced using yeast rather than human or animal cell lines. Similarly, an alternative for Polio is a vaccine known by the name IPOL, which is not derived from aborted tissue, nor is the vaccine Pediacel, an alternative to Pentacel, both of which are Polio Combination vaccines. The alternative for Mumps is Mumpsvax, for rabies is RabAvert and for measles is Attenuvax. The vaccines under these names are produced either from monkey kidney cells or chicken embryos. There are also vaccine alternatives available in the United Kingdom, which are not available in the United States because they are not FDA approved. For example, the alternative for Rubella is known as Takahashi Strain and the Hepatitis-A vaccine is known as Aimmugen. They are derived from rabbit and monkey kidney tissue respectively.

Vaccines and Religious Freedom

In addition to the problem of some vaccines derived from aborted tissue, there is a larger problem with mandatory vaccines. Many people have a sincerely held religious belief regarding vaccines in general. These individuals believe that God created the human body as a temple and that the body should not be destroyed by injecting a virus into it. Take, for example, Joseph and Heyde Rotella and Maja Leibovitz of New York City. Both families have a sincerely held religious belief against vaccinations. When the Rotellas had a seventh-grade daughter and Ms. Leibovitz had a second-grade daughter, the school system required that these children receive a mandatory Hepatitis-B vaccination. Hepatitis-B can only be transmitted in one of three ways. Either you are born to a mother with Hepatitis-B, or you contract it by drug use through the sharing of needles, or you contract it through sexual contact. Injecting their children with Hepatitis-B is like the state forcing the parents to give their children clean needles or condoms.

In both cases, the children were expelled from school, and in one case, Child Protective Services was called to the scene because the child was not in school. After several weeks of expulsion and threats of removing the children, Liberty Counsel filed a federal lawsuit. A court order allowed the children back in school and prohibited the school from overriding the parents' religious beliefs.

Some people have sincerely held religious beliefs against vaccines in general, while others have objections to certain vaccines because of their aborted fetal contents.

Liberty Counsel also filed a federal lawsuit against the state of Arkansas. There, the state requires mandatory vaccinations. Our clients have sincerely held religious beliefs opposing these mandatory vaccinations, including the chicken pox vaccination. One of our clients has actually received a letter from the Vatican stating that the Church opposes abortion and it would be a sin for the parent to allow her child to be injected with aborted fetal tissue. Despite the strong evidence of a religious belief which opposes the chicken pox vaccination, the state of Arkansas insisted that the parent vaccinate her child. Our federal lawsuit challenged the state's law on religious freedom grounds. As a result, the Arkansas legislature promptly acted to provide exemptions for philosophical and religious objectors, as well as objectors who claim medical necessity.

Hepatitis-B is not the only sexually transmitted disease for which states are currently trying to force parents to vaccinate their children. In 2006, the Centers for Disease Control [and Prevention, CDC] began recommending Gardasil, a vaccination created by Merck & Company, for vaccination against the Human Papillomavirus (HPV). Human Papillomavirus is a virus transmitted primarily through sexual contact. Rarely is there even a case where an infant contracts HPV from its mother. However, states like Michigan, Texas, California, and Kentucky have already attempted to mandate HPV vaccinations for girls entering sixth grade. Many parents have religious-based objections to mandatory vaccinations for viruses like Hepatitis-B and HPV, which should be prevented through abstinence.

No Legitimate Reason for Some Vaccines

Vaccinations are becoming a wave of the future. Large pharmaceutical companies are lobbying state legislators to require mandatory vaccinations of all school-aged children. Some people have sincerely held religious beliefs against vaccines in general, while others have objections to certain vaccines because of their aborted fetal contents. Either way, the state cannot steamroll a person's religious beliefs. In many cases, the government cannot even legitimately argue a compelling reason for the vaccines. Chicken pox is not life-threatening, Hepatitis-B is primarily contracted through drug use and sexual contact, and HPV is almost exclusively transmitted by sexual contact.

Next time you are confronted with mandatory vaccines, take a moment to reexamine your religious beliefs and become educated about the contents, the purpose, and the risk of vaccinations.

8

Noncompliance with Mandatory Vaccinations Threatens Community Health

Arthur Allen

Arthur Allen is a journalist and author of Vaccine: The Controversial Story of Medicine's Greatest Lifesaver.

Resistance to vaccinations is growing and many affluent, well-educated communities now have high percentages of unvaccinated children. People choose not to vaccinate their children for a variety of reasons, but one of the reasons the movement has grown recently is a fear that vaccines cause autism. The link between vaccines and autism has been scientifically disproven, but several celebrities have kept this and other fears alive. Given the harms risked by not vaccinating, to not vaccinate is selfish and puts the larger community at risk.

In the last trimester of her pregnancy, Helena Moran caught a cough that she couldn't get rid of. She figured she'd picked up the germ—whatever it was—from one of her patients at a Boulder dentist's office. But the real nightmare began after her daughter, Evelina, was born: The baby began to cough and cough, and then she'd curl up in a little ball and turn blue. At the emergency room, she was diagnosed with whooping cough. She spent the next five weeks in intensive care and suffered permanent lung damage.

Arthur Allen, "Immune to Reason: Are Vaccine Skeptics Putting Your Kids at Risk?" *Mother Jones*, vol. 33, no. 5, September/October 2008, pp. 91–92. Copyright © 2008 Foundation for National Progress. Reproduced by permission.

A Dangerous Movement

It turned out that by working in Boulder—one of the wealthiest, most well-educated towns in the country—Moran had put herself at risk of contracting a disease that largely disappeared after widespread vaccination against it began in the 1950s. Since the early 1990s, whooping cough has periodically whipped through Boulder, where a large percentage of parents do not immunize their children, public health officials say.

There's a Boulder in almost every state. Childhood vaccination rates nationwide are near record levels, in part thanks to a [President Bill] Clinton-era program that guarantees free vaccines for the poor. But as I learned while researching my book, *Vaccine*, a history of immunization, resistance is also growing, especially among affluent and well-educated people—to the point where living in a place with a high percentage of PhDs is a risk factor for whooping cough. "These are people who know better," UCLA whooping cough expert James Cherry told me, "but they don't know *enough*."

The point is to protect not merely ourselves, but the community.

Vaccine resisters are motivated by a range of convictions—immunization isn't "natural" (the wellness set), it's suspect because it's government mandated (Christian home-schoolers), and so on—but the movement got a huge boost from the controversy over the mercury-laden preservative thimerosal, which some theorized might be linked to autism. That link has been disproven—by, if nothing else, the fact that autism rates remained steady after pediatricians and public health authorities told manufacturers to stop making thimerosal-containing childhood vaccines in 1999. But the anti-vaccine movement has kept going, finding ever new reasons to distrust immunization. Some, including celebrity pediatrician Dr. Robert W. Sears, have raised fears about aluminum in the shots, while others—like the 2,000 or so protesters at a Washington rally this June [2008]—simply charge that kids get "too many vaccines" full of "dangerous toxins" that overwhelm their immune systems.

Celebrity over Science

The skeptics have many things going for them: our justifiable distrust of medical authority; our admiration for do-it-yourselfers, mavericks, and the self-taught; even a dose of celebrity appeal from the likes of Charlie Sheen, Jenny McCarthy, and Jim Carrey. What most of them don't have is an understanding of the science. Thanks to vaccines, polio and diphtheria are now pretty well confined to the world's medical backwaters. But tetanus lives everywhere in soil and rusty nails, and as many as 6 million Americans are exposed to whooping cough each year, according to surveys of blood antibodies. This year [2008], measles has returned, with the worst US outbreak since 2001. Most of the patients have been unvaccinated children and adults, and nearly a quarter have been hospitalized. In Third World countries with no measles vaccination, the disease killed nearly a quarter-million children in 2006.

Current medical practice is to vaccinate babies against whooping cough beginning at two months of age. Widespread vaccination creates "herd immunity"—the disease has fewer hosts, which means there are fewer people to spread it to those at serious risk, from immunocompromised adults (think chemotherapy patients) to newborns such as Evelina Moran and Teddy Hickenlooper, the infant son of Denver mayor John Hickenlooper, who caught whooping cough from an unvaccinated older child in 2002.

Vaccinating for the Community

Here's where we get to the deeper, fundamentally *progressive* reason for vaccination: The point is to protect not merely ourselves, but the community. To not vaccinate is to threaten the immunological commons, the array of trillions of antibodies and T cells that decades of vaccination have built up in our bodies, draping a web of germ-fighting agents around our most vulnerable neighbors. To not vaccinate is to affirm an overweening individuality. It's a form of selfishness.

Right now, in many states, all it takes to get an exemption from vaccine requirements is signing a form. Some, including a group of doctors at Johns Hopkins University, have proposed making it harder—allowing a philosophical exemption only after parents demonstrate a good-faith effort to educate themselves.

True, medical experts have failed us before; to make sure they are doing their job, we need to strongly support the public health programs whose job it is to watch out for serious adverse reactions to vaccines. But while questioning authority is healthy, facts are facts. If vaccines really were responsible for autism, it would be too much to ask parents to do the altruistic thing. But more than a dozen studies have failed to discover such a link—and not a single legitimate study has shown that one exists. I have spent many, many hours reading these studies and talking to vaccine scientists. I find no reason to believe Jim Carrey more than I believe them. Call me a dupe of the establishment, but I'd rather trust the doctors.

9

A Mandatory HPV Vaccine Will Create a Backlash

The Christian Science Monitor

The Christian Science Monitor is a national independent daily newspaper that seeks to provide context and clarity on national and international news, people, cultures, and social trends.

A new vaccine for the human papillomavirus, or HPV, shows promise in its potential to reduce the incidence of cervical cancer. Nonetheless, legislation that seeks to mandate the vaccine for school-aged girls is inappropriate at the present time. There are still questions about the safety and efficacy of the vaccine in the long term, and mandating the vaccine at this time could jeopardize parental compliance with all mandated vaccines. Parents should be allowed to choose what is best for their children. For some, this will mean choosing to have their daughters vaccinated, and for others, it will mean declining to do so. This decision must stay with the parents, because if this vaccine becomes mandatory, where will government intrusion stop?

If some state lawmakers around the country prevail, girls as young as 10 could soon face a mandatory medical appointment: They would need to be vaccinated against a sexually transmitted virus said to cause cancer—or risk being denied entrance to school.

Already 20 states are considering making the vaccine mandatory for preteen girls. In Texas, Gov. Rick Perry avoided a legislative debate with an executive order requiring all girls who will be sixth-graders in September 2008 to be vaccinated.

In most states, including Texas, parents who object on religious or medical grounds would be able to opt out. But why can't lawmakers reverse the process, letting those who want it "opt in" voluntarily?

Vaccinating Girls Against HPV

Doctors say the human papillomavirus is the leading cause of cervical cancer. Drug manufacturer Merck claims that the vaccine, called Gardasil, could eliminate 70 percent of cases of the disease if girls are vaccinated before becoming sexually active. The Food and Drug Administration [FDA] approved the vaccine in June [2006] for females between the ages of 9 and 26. Supporters are hailing the vaccine as a sure way to reduce deaths. But some doctors are urging caution.

Besides the estimated $360 cost for a series of three shots, the most pressing questions are moral and ethical, beginning with: Why the rush? And why the medical coercion?

If successful, these efforts would mark a shift in public-health policy. Until now, mandatory inoculations have been reserved for diseases regarded as communicable, representing a public health risk. Gardasil is designed to protect against a virus whose transmission can be prevented through individual behavior.

This decision belongs to parents, not state governments.

Side Effects of Gardasil

In addition, Merck is playing multiple roles. As the sole manufacturer of the vaccine, the pharmaceutical giant is waging an aggressive campaign to make its use mandatory. It is helping states such as Florida draft legislation. It is also giving money to Women in Government, a group working to require vaccinations. These efforts hardly represent altruism on the drugmaker's part. Merck stands to make billions of dollars if inoculations become mandatory.

The vaccine also is said to produce minor, temporary side effects. Since the FDA approved Gardasil last summer [2006], 82 girls and women have reported adverse reactions. Although Merck calls that number "small," no one knows the long-term effects. Among the 25,000 patients who took part in early tests, only 1,194—less than 5 percent—were preteen girls. That is hardly a reason to turn girls into medical guinea pigs.

One hopeful sign comes from Michigan, the first state to introduce such legislation. Lawmakers defeated the bill last month, saying the bill would interfere with family privacy.

Parents Should Choose

If this vaccine becomes mandatory, where will such government intrusion stop? If other vaccines become available, promising to prevent or cure noncommunicable diseases, might they, too, be required by law?

Caring parents everywhere want to do what they believe is best for their children. For some in this case, that will mean choosing to have their daughters vaccinated. For others, it will mean declining to do so. Either way, families deserve options, not coercion, in private health matters.

The decision belongs to parents, not state governments.

10

A Mandatory HPV Vaccine Will Save Lives

Ellen M. Daley and Robert J. McDermott

Ellen M. Daley is an assistant professor and Robert J. McDermott is a professor in Community and Family Health at the University of South Florida College of Public Health.

The new human papillomavirus (HPV) vaccine was developed to protect women from developing cervical cancer, a leading cause of death from cancer in women. There is a high likelihood of acquiring HPV without the vaccine, and some women with HPV will develop cervical cancer. Vaccinating against HPV at a young age has been shown to be safe and the most effective way of inoculating against HPV. Making the HPV vaccine mandatory for attendance at school is the best way to ensure that far fewer women die of cervical cancer. Just like other mandatory school vaccinations, it protects the individual and the community from serious disease.

In 1999, the *Morbidity and Mortality Weekly Report (MMWR)* identified the ten most significant public health achievements of the last 100 years. First on the list of accomplishments was vaccination, a biomedical and public health success story responsible for saving millions of lives and preventing untold misery from infectious diseases. Both life expectancy and quality of life have improved because of vaccines that

Ellen M. Daley and Robert J. McDermott, "The HPV Vaccine: Separating Politics from Science—a Commentary," *American Journal of Health Education*, vol. 38, no. 3, May/June 2007, pp. 177–79. Copyright © 2007 American Alliance for Health, Physical Education, Recreation and Dance. Reproduced by permission.

have eradicated diseases such as smallpox, and virtually eliminated childhood diseases such as measles, diphtheria and pertussis (whooping cough).

A particularly good example of the impact of vaccines are ones developed to combat infantile paralysis (polio), first by [Jonas] Salk, and later, by [Albert] Sabin. Between 1951 and 1954, immediately prior to the widespread dissemination of Salk's polio vaccine, there were over 16,000 cases of paralytic poliomyelitis, and an average of 1900 U.S. deaths annually from polio. The Salk vaccine was licensed in the U.S. in 1955, and cases of the disease dropped precipitously to fewer than 1000 per year until 1962, when the Sabin vaccine was licensed and administered on a widespread basis. By the end of 1962, fewer than 100 cases were seen annually. There has not been a naturally occurring case of polio in the United States since 1979. Concerted efforts by health and non-profit organizations to disseminate the polio vaccine have reduced the global burden of polio from approximately 350,000 cases per year in the late 1980s to 1200 cases in 2005, the 50th anniversary of the development of the vaccine.

Human Papillomavirus and Cancer

A new vaccine has been developed and released for use against a leading cause of death in women worldwide—cervical cancer. The human papillomavirus, or HPV, a species-specific DNA virus with over 100 types identified to date, has been recognized as the causal agent in the development of cervical cancer. It also is associated with other cancers (e.g., anal, penile, vulvar, vaginal, and oral-pharyngeal). Over 30 types of HPV are anogenital [of the anus and genitals], and approximately half of those are oncogenic [causing tumors]. If left untreated, they have the ability to progress to invasive cancers. Other anogenital HPV types, known as low-risk types, are responsible for genital warts. Whereas genital warts are benign, they are visible and may be a source of embarrassment. HPV is common—a recent U.S. study concluded that overall prevalence among 14–24-year-old women, an age group included in the age range targeted for the HPV vaccine, is 33.8%, and that: "This prevalence corresponds with 7.5 million females with HPV infection, which is higher than the previous estimate of 4.6 million prevalent HPV infections among females in this same age group in the United States." Furthermore, the lifetime likelihood of acquiring HPV is estimated to be 75% or more. Fortunately, infection with HPV also is transient, and in most cases, will clear up through the body's own immune response. According to the National Cancer Institute, about 10% of women have an oncogenic HPV infection at a given time, and they are more common in young women than in older women. Most cervical infections, including ones involving oncogenic types of HPV, clear on their own without causing cancer.

The decision to recommend that girls of ages 11–12 receive the vaccine is sound.

In the U.S., cervical cancer incidence and deaths have significantly decreased because of a well-designed and effective screening program, with an estimated number of 11,150 invasive cervical cancer cases, and 3,670 deaths forecast for 2007. Globally, the picture is grim as more than 250,000 women die annually from cervical cancer, making it the second most common cause of cancer death in women. Moreover, the World Health Organization anticipates a 25% increase in cervical cancer deaths over the next decade if significant interventions do not occur. In addition, 80% of the approximately half million women who will be diagnosed with cervical cancer worldwide live in resource-poor developing countries that do not have the infrastructure to provide cytology [the study of cells] screening for the disease. Even in the U.S., the nearly 3,700 women who will die of cervical cancer will have something in common—no screening or no treatment follow-up after screening. These facts speak to access to health care, and the conclusion is clear—cervical cancer is a disease of disparity. Women who are able to afford screening by Pap tests and HPV tests will not likely die of the disease. Rather, the women who lack access to screening and treatment become the victims of an otherwise largely preventable disease and cause of death.

Importance of the HPV Vaccine

The vaccine, which has passed through three phases of trials to receive licensure and approval from the U.S. Centers for Disease Control and Prevention's Advisory Committee on Immunization Practices (ACIP), has proven to be virtually 100% effective against the two types of HPV (types 16 and 18) responsible for some 70% of all cervical cancers. Both the Merck and the GlaxoSmithKline versions of the HPV vaccines have demonstrated that girls 10 to 15 years of age who received the vaccine prior to exposure to the virus have mounted stronger immune responses than girls and women 16 to 23 years of age in the clinical trials. This finding is one of the reasons that recommendations call for 11–12-year-old girls (possibly as young as age 9) to receive the vaccine at the health care provider's discretion. The vaccine appears to be safe, with only localized injection site reactions noted—an especially important factor in its development, because there is no HPV DNA in the vaccine, only virus-like particles (VLP) that stimulate production of antibodies against the proteins that surround the virus itself.

The decision to recommend that girls of ages 11–12 receive the vaccine is sound, based upon the science of the vaccine development, and bolstered by the practicalities of decades of successful vaccination programs. This age group is one that is still accessible as a cohort to receive widespread protection through school entry programs. Implementing the vaccine in this way guarantees that few adolescents will miss out on this protection, and those who do will benefit from herd immunity. Medical and public health professional associations have endorsed the vaccine, including the American College of Obstetrics and Gynecology, the American Academy of Pediatrics, the Society for Adolescent Medicine, and the American Cancer Society.

Mandating school entry immunization against HPV is fundamentally no different than vaccinating youngsters against a wide range of other diseases.

Criticism Is Unwarranted

One might assume that a well-documented, safe, and effective vaccine against the second leading cause of cancer death in women worldwide (the first anti-cancer vaccine of any kind for humans) not only would be hailed as *this* century's greatest public health achievement, but also would be disseminated with lightning speed. Regrettably, such accolade and action cannot be taken for granted. The debate over mandatory school entry vaccination is in full cry nationwide. Whereas some caution is called for in any new achievement that affects the public's health, *this* immunization program, unfortunately, is linked to a sexually transmitted virus. Thus, we propose two questions for readers' consideration: (1) If this vaccine were approved for a virus that was non-genital, or not associated with sexual behavior, would we see delay in its deployment? and (2) If this vaccine combated a virus that caused precancerous and cancerous conditions in boys and men only, would we be confronted with the same level of controversy and reticence about its deployment? There is something fundamentally uncomfortable to Americans who might have to consider that adolescent girls, especially if they are their own daughters, will become sexually active and acquire a sexually transmitted virus. Now is not the time to avoid issues that may be linked to emotions or discomfort. Some women will die of this disease, and at least 70% of those deaths could be prevented through administration of procedures similar to those that have eradicated smallpox and minimized the public health threat of polio and numerous other viral diseases.

Because this virus is transmitted through sexual contact, we are at risk of losing an opportunity to achieve equity in protection against a condition related to poverty and lack of access to care. Vaccinating adolescent girls before they encounter this virus will save thousands, and globally, hundreds of thousands, of lives. Mandating school entry immunization against HPV is fundamentally no different than vaccinating youngsters against a wide range of other diseases. Parental consent and "opt out" choices are important, but education about the vaccine is critical for allaying fears. Therefore, health care providers, health educators, and other personnel must reach out to describe the vaccine's safety and effectiveness. If this vaccine is to gain status as the public health achievement of at least the early portion of the current century—we need to move the debate away from antecedent behaviors and advance the vaccine message for preventing unnecessary cancer deaths.

11

A Mandatory HPV Vaccine Encourages Sex and Poses Other Problems

Michael Fumento

Michael Fumento is an author, journalist, photographer, and attorney specializing in science and health issues. He is the author of BioEvolution: How Biotechnology Is Changing Our World.

There are several concerns about making the human papillomavirus (HPV) vaccine mandatory for school-aged girls. The vaccine is different from other vaccines because it protects against a disease acquired by sexual activity. There is a legitimate concern that inoculating young girls could send the message that sexual activity is permissible. Furthermore, the risk of cervical cancer from HPV, combined with advanced screening techniques, makes the argument for urgent vaccination dubious, especially when examining the recent activities of Merck, the manufacturer of the Gardasil vaccine. The vaccine may be useful, but these concerns need to be taken into account.

Legislators in some 20 states are considering making mandatory Merck & Co.'s Gardasil vaccination for the human papillomavirus [HPV]. In Texas, Republican governor Rick Perry bypassed the legislature and ordered it on his own. The requirement there applies to 11- and 12-year-old girls entering 6th grade. [This legislation was overturned by the legislature in May 2007.]

The benefits seem clear. FDA [Food and Drug Administration]-approved for females age 9 to 26, the vaccine has been shown to be 100 percent effective at preventing disease from the two HPV strains that account for 70 percent of all cervical cancers. Government estimates are that there will be 11,150 cases and 3,670 deaths from cervical cancer in 2007. So what's not to like?

Plenty.

The HPV Vaccine Is Different

One argument is that a mandate removes parental authority. Which it does, but so do all mandatory vaccinations. The difference here is that while Perry claims the HPV vaccine is no different from the polio vaccine, polio is transmitted through the breath, while HPV is transmitted by sexual intercourse.

As Robert Zavoski, physician and president of the Connecticut chapter of the American Academy of Pediatrics, explained to the *Hartford Courant*, "Vaccines previously mandated for universal use are those which protect the public's health against agents easily communicated, responsible for epidemics, or causing significant morbidity or mortality among those passively exposed to the illness." He added, "HPV is not an agent of this sort."

> *When you insist that 11-year-old girls receive shots to protect them from dangers attending sexual intercourse, you are sending them a message.*

The other argument, which many Christian groups have made in addition to the one about parental authority, is that a mandatory vaccination will encourage promiscuity. This idea has been mocked. District of Columbia councilman David Catania, sponsor of a mandatory HPV vaccine bill, for example, insists, "This vaccine no more encourages sexual activity than a tetanus shot encourages you to step on a rusty nail."

But again, the analogy is faulty. There is no biological urge to step on rusty nails. There is, however, a powerful urge to have sexual intercourse that begins at puberty. It's an urge that nations and religions throughout history have sought to control in various ways because sexual intercourse, while pleasurable to the participants at the time, can have consequences that are deleterious to the individuals later as well as to society as a whole.

When you insist that 11-year-old girls receive shots to protect them from dangers attending sexual intercourse, you are sending them a message. In fact, you're even sending their male peers a message. And it is one that conflicts with the message that sexual activity is best left to people who are more mature.

The Risk of Cancer

Still, what about those preventable infections and cancers? HPV infection is usually fairly benign; in fact, a study just released [2007] by the CDC [Centers for Disease Control and Prevention] says about 27 percent of U.S. females aged 14 to 59 years have it. Importantly, only 2.2 percent of those women are carrying one of the two virus strains most likely to lead to cervical cancer. Usually infection is asymptomatic; but in a minority of cases it leads to tiny cauliflower-like bumps on the genitalia (or anus) that will disappear on their own or be zapped off by a doctor. And in a much smaller minority of cases, infection leads to cell irregularities that become cervical cancer.

The 3,670 deaths from cervical cancer expected this year are a tiny fraction of the 270,100 projected female deaths from all cancers. Further, both the incidence and the death rate for cervical cancer are dropping. The incidence was 14.8 per 100,000 women in 1973 according to federal data, but down to 7.1 per 100,000 by 2003. Meanwhile, the incidence of cancer generally increased. "Cervical cancer was the only cancer among the top 15 cancers that decreased in women of all races and ethnicities," according to the American Cancer Society. Cervical cancer death rates declined steadily from 5.6 per 100,000 in 1975 to 2.5 in 2003.

Psychology must be considered as well as physiology.

The main reason for the declines in both incidence and death is the Pap test or Pap smear. Public health campaigns and individual physicians have sought to convince women to get these tests, in which tiny samples are scraped from the opening of the cervix. Moreover, computer imaging has improved the reading of these smears, leading to fewer false results. Early treatment has also improved, with the use of a laser to vaporize cells showing abnormal growth.

Pap smears are not 100 percent effective at finding cells before they become cancerous, but they have the added benefit of detecting pre-cancerous cells with causes other than HPV. These include other sexually transmitted diseases. Remember, too, that Gardasil prevents only 70 percent of HPV infections that lead to cervical cancer. Thus, even women who have been vaccinated must still be encouraged to get Pap smears every three years.

Yet if the Gardasil inoculation sends a message about intercourse, it also sends a much stronger message about Pap smears. Why bother when one is already protected (mostly) from the big danger, cervical cancer? Psychology must be considered as well as physiology.

Latency Period

The usefulness of detection programs is enhanced by the long latency time from HPV infection to cancer. According to physician Mark Spitzer, a gynecologist at New York Methodist Hospital, in a small minority of women, "viral persistence may result in the development of a carcinoma in situ [remaining within the cervix] lesion about 8 or 9 years later. The transition from carcinoma in situ to microinvasive cancer takes a long time, since the median age of microinvasive cancer is approximately 41, or about 12 years older than carcinoma in situ. The median age of [potentially lethal] invasive carcinoma is not for another 7 years after that."

Do the math. After an initial latency period of, say, 8 months (but possibly "many years or decades"), add an additional 8 years, plus 12 more years, plus 7 more years before we have a life-threatening, invasive carcinoma—28 years total. That's why the age bracket with the highest rate of death from cervical cancer is 45–54 and the second highest is 55–64. HPV is generally a young woman's disease; cervical cancer generally that of older women. Averages, of course, are just that. Some will develop the cancer sooner and others later. But once you realize we're talking about an almost three-decade-long period that doesn't begin until the woman first has intercourse and becomes infected, the speed with which politicians are trying to foist these mandates upon parents seems unwarranted.

Indeed, cervical cancer could conceivably be a thing of the past before today's young vaccine candidates reach middle age. As computers become more powerful—with developments such as Intel's "teraflop chip," Hewlett-Packard's nanochip, and even quantum computing—drug and biologic testing will be transformed, made vastly faster and more effective. Yet as long ago as 1999, a CDC representative testified before Congress that with then-current medical technology and heightened awareness of the need for Pap smears, cervical cancer was "nearly 100 percent preventable."

Shady Dealings

So why such urgency on the part of lawmakers? Maybe it reflects urgency on the part of Gardasil's maker, Merck & Co. [In December 2006], at a briefing on Wall Street, the president of global human health at Merck, Peter Loescher, remarked that he stresses "speed, speed, speed" in a product launch. That may be because another HPV vaccine, Cervarix from GlaxoSmithKline [GSK], was submitted to the European Union for approval [in early 2006], and GSK is expected to submit it to the FDA [in 2007].

Moreover, in January [2007] GSK announced a head-to-head clinical trial against Gardasil, indicating it believes it may have a superior product. In any event, Cervarix would certainly cut into the profit margin of Merck's vaccine, which, at $360 for the series of three inoculations, is the most expensive vaccine available.

To that end, "Merck is bankrolling efforts to pass state laws across the country," according to the Associated Press [AP]. The *Baltimore Sun* was the first to report that Women in Government, a national advocacy group of female state legislators that's been lobbying hard for mandatory Gardasil vaccinations, has been taking Merck money. "In addition to vaccination mandates, Merck supports measures that would require private insurers and Medicaid to cover the cost of the vaccine," said the *Sun*. The paper also relayed the estimates of Wall Street analysts: "The vaccine is expected to reach $1 billion in sales next year, and state mandates could make Gardasil a mega-blockbuster drug within five years, with sales of more than $4 billion."

The real need for an HPV vaccine is outside the United States.

The AP meanwhile reported it obtained documents showing Gov. Perry's chief of staff met with key aides about Gardasil the same day its manufacturer donated money to Perry's campaign. That day, Merck's political action committee forked over $5,000 to Perry and $5,000 total to eight state lawmakers.

"It's not the vaccine community pushing for this," physician Martin Myers, director of the National Network for Immunization Information, told the *Sun*. Myers, former head of the federal National Vaccine Program Office, added, "Many of us are concerned a mandate may be premature, and it's important for people to realize that this isn't as clear-cut as with some previous vaccines."

Finally, in the face of all this bad publicity, Merck announced it would stop lobbying for mandatory vaccination.

Going Slow with the Vaccine

In any event, the real need for an HPV vaccine is outside the United States. According to the World Health Organization, cervical cancer worldwide strikes half a million women yearly and kills 250,000 of them. In developing countries it is the greatest cause of cancer deaths in women. There, neither incidence nor death rates are falling. WHO has also found that "cervical cancer screening programs in [Latin America and the Caribbean] have generally failed to reduce cases and mortality rates largely because of inadequacies in treatment and follow-up." That's where these vaccines need to go, with support from such philanthropies as the Bill and Melinda Gates Foundation. Obviously, though, the price will have to come way down from that $360.

None of this is to deny that HPV vaccines have the potential to save lives and possibly also money in the U.S. market—though cost considerations must take into account that under a mandatory program, we would be shelling out $360 per vaccine for tens of millions of people. This is not to say these vaccines shouldn't continue to be available to women and parents who feel they can afford them. It is to say we can afford to wait for Merck to receive some healthy competition. Nor should the concerns of those worried about both the loss of parental control and the encouragement of early sexual intercourse be dismissed so lightly.

12

A Mandatory HPV Vaccine Will Not Encourage Sexual Activity

Meghan O'Rourke

Meghan O'Rourke is a writer and poet and Slate's *culture critic.*

The opposition to the human papillomavirus (HPV) vaccine based on concerns about condoning and promoting sexual activity is ignorant and irrational. HPV can be acquired by just one sexual encounter, making HPV a disease that affects everyone, not just the promiscuous. In addition, there is no reason to think the vaccine will increase sexual activity. The reason this concern materialized is likely due to the recommended age of eleven or twelve for administering the vaccines, an age when young girls are just reaching puberty. Had the vaccines been recommended for childhood, the worry about sexual activity probably would not have arisen.

In recent months, you may have seen a TV ad featuring striking young women skateboarding and drumming as a voice-over intones, "Every year, thousands of women die from cervical cancer. I want to be one less woman who will battle cancer." The women represented are self-confident, accomplished, artistic, and independent. Only one boy shows up in the ad—in a still photo. But what is most striking about the ad is that it is just one part of a much larger cultural and political battle about young women and sex.

Opposition to the HPV Vaccine

America declared a "war on cancer" 30 years ago, and yet few cures or vaccines have been discovered since. So when Merck announced that it had created a drug that could prevent some 70 percent of cervical cancers from developing, you would think Americans would rejoice. Instead, there was a backlash. Last February [2007], Republican Gov. Rick Perry signed an executive order that would have made Texas the first state to mandate the vaccination of schoolgirls against HPV, the sexually transmitted virus that is a frequent cause of cervical cancer. He promptly came under fierce attack. The Texas Legislature expressed its deep reservations about the vaccine, and the media reported that Perry had received a campaign contribution from Merck prior to signing the order. Ultimately, the order was vetoed by the legislature. Earlier this year [2007], 24 states were contemplating making Gardasil—as the cervical-cancer vaccine is known—a mandatory vaccination for young women. Today, only one state, Virginia, has such a law, and it leaves a loophole for parents to opt out.

In one sense, this reluctance seems understandable. Merck is the same company that made headlines in 2004 for failing to disclose that its painkiller Vioxx raised the risk of cardiac arrest and stroke in patients. Gardasil is a brand-new drug, and the company has conducted only limited testing on it. Though the pre-release studies suggest it is highly efficacious, the vaccine's long-term side effects are not fully known. What's more, the vaccination comprises three painful shots, at an estimated cost of $360. Given all this, it is hard to blame parents who resist putting their daughters on the drug's front line, preferring to wait until more is known about it.

Much less understandable, though, is the position taken by many opponents: namely, that a cervical-cancer vaccination would "promote promiscuity" among teenage girls. Implicit in this argument is the assumption that good girls don't get cervical cancer; only "loose" ones do—and they may get what they deserve. Earlier [in 2007], State Sen. George Runner of California told the *Los Angeles Times* that American money would be much better spent on other types of vaccines, since cervical cancer is a result of lifestyle choices, rather than bad genetic luck.

The idea that a mere vaccination could "promote promiscuity" is bizarrely simplistic.

The Concern About Sexual Activity

This view involves a hefty dose of ignorance, as well as a dollop of old-fashioned magical thinking. As any doctor can tell you, it takes only one sexual contact to contract a strain of HPV that can lead to cervical cancer. The CDC [Centers for Disease Control and Prevention] reports that at least 50 percent of Americans are infected with HPV over the course of their lives, and a whopping 80 percent of American women are infected by age 50. Admittedly, the chances are slim that HPV would lead to cervical cancer: Only a small portion of HPV infections become cancerous. Still, according to the National Cancer Institute, roughly 11,000 women will be diagnosed with cervical cancer this year in the United States. Nearly 3,700 women will die. If you are one of those 3,700 women, you might feel that a vaccine could have changed everything. And—contrary to Runner's insinuations—you needn't be a slut to be among them: You could have married a guy who slept with just one other girl. Or, of course, you could be one of the approximately 13 percent of American women who, according to a 2003 study, are or will be a victim of rape over the course of their lives.

Meanwhile, the idea that a mere vaccination could "promote promiscuity" is bizarrely simplistic—as if the prick of a needle in the arm of a pre-adolescent girl stands in for a, well, prick of another kind. For one thing, no evidence suggests a connection between a decrease in HPV and an increase in sexual activity, nor is it likely to: HPV is hardly a major deterrent to kids who might be squeamish about STDs [sexually transmitted diseases], since it has few short-term effects and cervical cancer usually takes years to develop. Adolescents have a hard enough time thinking about next week, let alone a decade from now. They're more likely to be worried about the immediate effects of herpes, gonorrhea, or syphilis, or even AIDS, which is still more prevalent than cervical cancer. For another thing, there's already a vaccine out there designed to prevent a sexually transmitted disease—and *it's* not being protested by anyone on the grounds that it might encourage promiscuity. That vaccine is for hepatitis B, and it is given to approximately 88 percent of all American children by the time they are 19 months old. Finally, it's not as if adolescents are incredibly rational about their sexual calculations, as the vaccine-promiscuity argument would have Americans believe.

Even if the vaccination did encourage promiscuity, it's not clear that it's OK for women to die as a result.

An Age Problem

On the contrary, the reason so many legislators and parents have conjured up a tie between vaccination and sex clearly has less to do with objective reality than with the age at which girls are supposed to receive the vaccine. Gov. Perry's executive order would have mandated that girls receive the vaccine as they go into sixth grade, at age 11 or 12—precisely the juncture between childhood and adulthood we're the most uncertain about how to conceptualize. According to Sydney Spiesel, a pediatrician and a *Slate* writer, parents often complain that 11 is too early for a Gardasil shot, because their daughters aren't sexually active yet. But that's not the point; the point is that these pre-adolescents need to receive the vaccine well before they *are* sexually active.

It may be that Merck miscalculated in not finding a way for vaccinations to begin in childhood rather than in pre-adolescence, even if it meant patients needing a booster series. The later age encourages parents and politicians to make a categorical error, associating Gardasil with the pill or with the sex talk, when it needn't be associated at all (just as hep-B shots aren't). Merck may also have miscalculated by recommending that the vaccine be administered only to girls, though boys are carriers of HPV, too—and in fact, scientists believe that the virus plays a role in head and neck cancers as well as anal cancer. Merck is currently testing the drug for boys, but by now the debate has fully catalyzed pre-existing latent anxieties about young women and sex.

Hysteria Surrounding the Debate

Indeed, one of the most fascinating elements of the Gardasil debate is that the hysteria appears to have been internalized by some of the constituents themselves—a twist [psychiatrist Sigmund] Freud might appreciate. Rumors abound about significant negative side effects, although pre-release statistics show nothing out of the ordinary. (To be sure, early studies may not capture the full range of drug-related risks.) At one school in Australia, 26 girls injected with Gardasil went to the campus medical office complaining of adverse effects; a couple were hospitalized. Since then, additional reports of group dizziness and fainting have been posted in the comments section of various Internet sites. Since many patients now know the vaccine is controversial, one has to wonder whether some of these instances have more to do with sublimated anxiety about sex and with sociogenic effects than with the drug itself. (Spiesel said that none of his patients had reacted adversely, though he had heard of one case where a patient had.)

And so liberal parents who distrust Big Pharma are also highly suspicious of Gardasil. But as Darshak Sanghavi, a pediatric cardiologist and a *Slate* writer, told me, speaking by phone from his office, "Looking at the science, I think it's highly unlikely that there is any significant side effect that hasn't been caught. For sure, there could be something rare. But there is no suggestion of anything masked." He stressed the importance of contextualizing the vaccine, pointing out that it takes a lot of research money to create vaccines, and it is not always a profitable enterprise. Given the very real dangers of cervical cancer, Sanghavi said, "I don't believe that they have pushed [Gardasil] in an unethical manner. They have a product that is almost certainly going to save lives." In the meantime, fears about the health risks of Gardasil have obscured the hidden moral calculus of the conservative opposition to Gardasil: that in the end, it may be worth it for several thousand women to die from cervical cancer every year as collateral damage in the war against premarital teen sex. Because, of course, even if the vaccination *did* encourage promiscuity, it's not clear that it's OK for women to die as a result.

Protesters in all camps of the anti-vaccine coalition are chafing at what they see as the paternalism inherent in making vaccines mandatory. But if anyone in the government is being paternalistically intrusive, it's not the Gov. Perrys of the world. It's the legislators who are pursuing the war against premarital teen sex when they could seize the chance to eradicate the HPV virus and its associated cancers from the lives of young Americans. On second thought, this isn't really paternalistic at all. To pretend for a little longer that their daughters will never grow up, and that we all can protect them by hiding our heads in the sand for another few years—actually, that's just childish.

13

The HPV Vaccine Should Be Optional

Jesse Walker

Jesse Walker is the managing editor of Reason *magazine.*

State proposals to mandate the human papillomavirus (HPV) vaccine are misguided and should be opposed. Regardless of whether or not making the vaccine mandatory would ever be a good idea, it certainly is unwise to mandate it before some time has passed to assess the vaccine's safety and effectiveness. Furthermore, HPV is different from measles and other diseases prevented by current mandatory vaccinations because it is not easily contagious in a school setting. For this reason, the HPV vaccine should not be mandatory. People should be given the option to have the vaccine (an opt-in system) rather than the option to have an exception to a mandate (an opt-out system).

Gardasil isn't exactly an anti-cancer vaccine, but it comes close. It protects girls and women against four sexually transmitted strains of the human papillomavirus (HPV), two of which cause about 70 percent of all cervical cancer. It is also extremely controversial, though the nature of the controversy has changed radically since the treatment was invented. This time last year [in 2006] the issue was whether it would be allowed at all, a matter settled in June [2006] when the Food and Drug Administration [FDA] approved it. Today the question is whether the shots should be required.

State Proposals to Mandate Gardasil

Nearly half the states have been considering measures to mandate the vaccine for schoolchidren, with Texas Gov. Rick Perry skipping the debate entirely by issuing an executive order which, he insists, cannot be repealed by the legislature [but was repealed in May 2007]. In Michigan, by contrast, such a bill was shot down in January [2007], and in Maryland the proposal was withdrawn before it reached a vote.

Good for Michigan, good for Maryland, and too bad for Texas. The arguments against legalizing Gardasil were silly. The arguments against mandating it are strong.

Even Jonas Salk's celebrated polio vaccine, licensed in 1955, was not immediately required by any state.

Since the viruses it protects against are transmitted sexually, Gardasil is most effective when given to people who are not yet sexually active; scientists therefore recommend that girls aged 10 to 14 receive it. Opponents initially argued that this might encourage preteen promiscuity. But the point of early immunization is to protect people *before* sex is likely to be an issue—and even a woman committed to avoiding all sex before marriage might still contract the virus via rape, or by marrying a man who has not been as chaste as she. Contrary to certain popular stereotypes, the leaders of the religious right are not all imbeciles; well before the FDA approved Gardasil, groups like the Family Research Council had endorsed the shots, arguing only that the decision to vaccinate should be left in the hands of the families, not the state.

To be clear, a majority of the proposed laws, including the Texas order, are not completely compulsory. Most states allow families to refuse vaccinations on religious grounds, and some extend that exemption to parents with broader objections as well. The details vary from place to place, but in general, the shots would be more of a default setting than an absolute mandate. Even so, there are good reasons to oppose the proposals.

Why the Rush?

There are really two debates here: whether to require the vaccine at all, and whether to require it *now*. We'll begin with the second, more moderate question. Just as the Family Research Council refrained from fighting FDA approval of Gardasil [in 2006], the mainstream position in the medical community has been against compulsory HPV vaccines. When Gov. Perry's order was announced, the head of the Texas Medical Association informed the *Houston Chronicle* that "we don't support a state mandate at this time." Martin Myers, director of the National Network for Immunization Information, has told the *Baltimore Sun* that "a mandate may be premature, and it's important for people to realize that this isn't as clear-cut as with some previous vaccines." The American Academy of Pediatrics has endorsed the routine vaccination of 11- to 12-year-old girls against HPV but has not called for making the routine a requirement. And the American Academy of Family Physicians has officially adopted the position that "it is premature to consider school entry mandates for human papillomavirus vaccine ... until such time as the long term safety with widespread use, stability of supply, and economic issues have been clarified."

It's important to understand that all the people and organizations I just quoted are enthusiastic about the vaccine itself, and that most of them will probably support a mandate a few years down the road. What alarms them is the rush. "In the past," *Vaccine* author Arthur Allen pointed out, "public health authorities usually waited a few to several years before requiring children to get a new vaccine. For example, Merck's chickenpox vaccine, licensed in 1995, did not become mandatory in many states until 1999. The time between licensing and requirement allowed vaccine authorities time to view the safety and effectiveness record of the new vaccine before they ordered children to receive it. Even Jonas Salk's celebrated polio vaccine, licensed in 1955, was not immediately required by any state—though almost the entire country viewed polio as a menace to be battled together."

So who's campaigning to compel the shots? Mostly it's Merck, which—surprise!—manufactures the vaccine. In addition to its direct lobbying, the pharmaceutical giant donates money to Women in Government, an organization of female state legislators that has embraced the mandates. (Also, for whatever it's worth, Texas Gov. Perry's former chief of staff now works for Merck.) The company is also pushing for laws requiring insurers to pay for the shots.

[HPV] is 100 percent avoidable in the activities you're supposed to perform in the course of a school day.

Merck doesn't merely stand to gain if the government requires us to use its product. It stands to gain if politicians mandate the shots sooner rather than later. Another company, GlaxoSmithKline, is working on an HPV vaccine of its own, called Cervarix; it hopes to have it on the market [in 2007]. The Texas proclamation does not mention Gardasil by name, and it could be construed to cover future HPV vaccines as well. But obviously, enacting the law now will give Merck's market share a boost when the competition arrives.

The HPV Vaccine Should Be Opt-In

Which leads to the next question: Even if the vaccination isn't compulsory now, should it be obligatory sometime down the road? The knee-jerk libertarian reaction is to say no, and at least one of my knees is a confirmed libertarian. But there are circumstances under which it makes sense to require a vaccine. When a deadly disease can be spread through casual contact, a school would arguably be negligent *not* to require students to be inoculated against it, just as it would be negligent not to ensure that its roof won't collapse on the children beneath it. The more people are vaccinated, the less likely it is that any of them will transmit the illness. This is especially important when some of the parties present are medically ineligible for the vaccine, as some children inevitably are.

But you don't transmit these strains of HPV by breathing on a playmate or by leaving some spittle on a water fountain. You transmit them through intimate contact. It isn't entirely true, as some opponents of the mandates have carelessly claimed, that HPV is "100 percent avoidable"—not unless they mean avoiding sex your entire life. But it *is* 100 percent avoidable in the activities you're supposed to perform in the course of a school day. A person with HPV is not a clear and present danger the way a person with measles or whooping cough is.

Indeed, it was the co-creator of the measles vaccine, Samuel Katz, who argued in *USA Today* [in February 2007] that HPV "isn't transmitted in a classroom to dozens of children. It's not the same thing as infectious diseases that fly through the air with no boundaries." (Katz also declared that a mandate would "just throw oil on the flames of the anti-vaccine folks," creating a backlash that could hurt every vaccination effort.) The bioethicist Bernard Lo struck a similar note [in 2006] in *BMJ* [*British Medical Journal*], observing that "the rationale for mandatory vaccination is weaker for HPV than for childhood infections because HPV is not contagious."

As I noted before, most of the proposals being debated would not make the vaccinations absolutely mandatory; families who want to avoid them can find ways to do so. But an opt-in approach is vastly preferable to the opt-out option. It would mean that doctors will have to persuade parents to accept the shots: explaining the benefits, answering their questions, letting them know what other measures they should take to avoid cervical cancer, and, in general, giving them the autonomy and respect that they deserve. To people of a certain mindset—call them the therapeutic state, call them social engineers, call them something ruder—this is a roadblock to public health. But in fact it makes us healthier. It means more knowledgeable patients, more involvement in our own care, more trust between doctors and their clients. Outside of emergency conditions, it should be the norm.

Organizations to Contact

The editors have compiled the following list of organizations concerned with the issues debated in this book. The descriptions are derived from materials provided by the organizations. All have publications or information available for interested readers. The list was compiled on the date of publication of the present volume; the information provided here may change. Be aware that many organizations take several weeks or longer to respond to inquiries, so allow as much time as possible.

Association of American Physicians and Surgeons (AAPS)
1601 N. Tucson Blvd., Suite 9, Tucson, AZ   85716-3450
(800) 635-1196 • (520) 325-4230
e-mail: aaps@aapsonline.org
Web site: www.aapsonline.org

AAPS is a national association of physicians dedicated to preserving freedom in the one-on-one patient-physician relationship. AAPS fights in the courts for the rights of patients and physicians, sponsors seminars for physicians, testifies before committees in Congress, and educates the public. Among the news briefs and publications available at the AAPS Web site are a fact sheet on mandatory vaccines and the organization's resolution concerning mandatory vaccines.

Centers for Disease Control and Prevention (CDC)
1600 Clifton Rd., Atlanta, GA   30333
(800) 232-4636
e-mail: cdcinfo@cdc.gov
Web site: www.cdc.gov

The CDC, a part of the U.S. Department of Health and Human Services, is the primary federal agency conducting and supporting public health activities in the United States. Through research and education, the CDC is dedicated to protecting health and promoting quality of life through the prevention and control of disease, injury, and disability. Among the many publications available on the CDC's Web site regarding vaccines and immunizations are childhood, adolescent, and adult immunization schedules; information about reasons to vaccinate and the importance of vaccinating; and vaccine safety reports, including access to the Vaccine Adverse Event Reporting System (VAERS).

The Commonwealth Fund
1 E. Seventy-fifth St., New York, NY   10021
(212) 606-3800 • fax: (212) 606-3500
e-mail: info@cmwf.org
Web site: www.commonwealthfund.org

The Commonwealth Fund is a private foundation that aims to promote a high-performing health care system that achieves better patient access, improved quality, and greater efficiency, particularly for society's most vulnerable populations, including low-income people, the uninsured, minority Americans, young children, and elderly adults. The Commonwealth Fund carries out this mandate by supporting independent research on health care issues and making grants to improve health care practice and policy. The foundation publishes the *Commonwealth Fund Digest* and offers performance snapshots, including one on the issue of immunizing young children, available on its Web site.

Immunization Action Coalition (IAC)
1573 Selby Ave., Suite 234, St. Paul, MN   55104
(651) 647-9009 • fax: (651) 647-9131
e-mail: admin@immunize.org
Web site: www.immunize.org

The IAC works to increase immunization rates and prevent disease and creates educational materials and facilitates communication about the safety, efficacy, and use of vaccines within the broad immunization community of patients, parents, health care organizations, and government health agencies. The IAC publishes numerous brochures and vaccination schedules, including the brochure, "What If You Don't Immunize Your Child?"

Institute for Vaccine Safety (IVS)
Johns Hopkins Bloomberg School of Public Health
615 N. Wolfe St., Room W5041, Baltimore, MD   21205
(410) 955-2955 • fax: (410) 502-6733
e-mail: info@hopkinsvaccine.org
Web site: www.vaccinesafety.edu

IVS aims to obtain and disseminate objective information about the safety of recommended immunizations. It provides a forum for dissemination of data regarding specific issues concerning the safety of immunizations, investigates safety questions, and conducts research. IVS also sponsors academic publications about vaccination and provides information about state school vaccination law exemptions and vaccine legislation.

National Network for Immunization Information (NNii)
301 University Blvd., Galveston, TX   77555-0350
(409) 772-0199 • fax: (409) 772-5208
e-mail: nnii@i4ph.org
Web site: www.immunizationinfo.org

NNii is affiliated with the Infectious Diseases Society of America, the Pediatric Infectious Diseases Society, the American Academy of Pediatrics, the American Nurses Association, the American Academy of Family Physicians, the National Association of Pediatric Nurse Practitioners, the American College of Obstetricians and Gynecologists, the University of Texas Medical Branch, the Society for Adolescent Medicine, and the American Medical Association. NNii provides the public, health professionals, policy makers, and the media with up-to-date immunization information to help clarify the issues and help people make informed decisions regarding immunization. NNii publishes numerous briefs, papers, and pamphlets, including "Do Multiple Vaccines Overwhelm the Immune System?" available on its Web site.

National Vaccine Information Center (NVIC)

407 Church St., Suite H, Vienna, VA   22180
(703) 938-0342 • fax: (703) 938-5768
e-mail: contactnvic@gmail.com
Web site: www.nvic.org

NVIC is dedicated to defending the right to informed consent to medical interventions and to preventing vaccine injuries and deaths through public education. NVIC provides assistance to those who have suffered vaccine reactions; promotes research to evaluate vaccine safety and effectiveness; and monitors vaccine research, development, regulation, policy making and legislation. Many resources are available on NVIC's Web site, including position papers and articles, among which is "Promoting Vaccination, Fear, Hate & Discrimination."

Thinktwice Global Vaccine Institute

PO Box 9638, Santa Fe, NM   87504
(505) 983-1856
e-mail: global@thinktwice.com
Web site: www.thinktwice.com

The Thinktwice Global Vaccine Institute was established in 1996 to provide parents and other concerned people with educational resources to help them make more-informed vaccine decisions. Thinktwice encourages an uncensored exchange of vaccine information and supports every family's right to accept or reject vaccines. The institute offers various studies, articles, and books on its Web site, including the *Vaccine Safety Manual for Concerned Families and Health Practitioners.*

Vaccine Education Center

The Children's Hospital of Philadelphia
Thirty-fourth St. and Civic Center Blvd.
Philadelphia, PA   19104
(215) 590-9990
e-mail: vacinfo@email.chop.edu
Web site: www.vaccine.chop.edu

The Vaccine Education Center at the Children's Hospital of Philadelphia educates parents and health care providers about vaccines and immunizations. The center provides videos, informational tear sheets, and other information about every vaccine. Among these numerous publications available for download on the center's Web site is "Too Many Vaccines? What You Should Know."

Vaccine Liberation
PO Box 457, Spirit Lake, Idaho   83869-0457
(888) 249-1421
e-mail: vaclib@coldreams.com
Web site: www.vaclib.org

Vaccination Liberation is part of a national grassroots network dedicated to providing information, not often made available to the public, about vaccinations, with the goal of encouraging people to avoid and refuse vaccines. Vaccination Liberation works to dispute claims that vaccines are necessary, safe, and effective; expand awareness of alternatives in health care; preserve the right to abstain from vaccination; and repeal all compulsory vaccination laws nationwide. The organization offers various publications on its Web site, including "How to Legally Avoid School Immunizations."

Bibliography

Books

Arthur Allen   *Vaccine: The Controversial Story of Medicine's Greatest Lifesaver.* New York: Norton, 2007.

James Colgrove   *State of Immunity: The Politics of Vaccination in Twentieth-Century America.* Berkeley and Los Angeles: University of California Press, 2006.

Charles Creighton   *The Vaccination Myth: Courageous MD Exposes the Vaccination Fraud!.* Scotts Valley, CA: CreateSpace, 2009.

Lauren Feder   *The Parents' Concise Guide to Childhood Vaccinations: Practical Medical and Natural Ways to Protect Your Child.* Long Island City, NY: Hatherleigh Press, 2007.

Madelon Lubin Finkel   *Truth, Lies, and Public Health: How We Are Affected When Science and Politics Collide.* Westport, CT: Praeger, 2007.

David Kirby   *Evidence of Harm: Mercury in Vaccines and the Autism Epidemic: A Medical Controversy.* New York: St. Martin's, 2005.

Kurt Link   *The Vaccine Controversy: The History, Use, and Safety of Vaccinations.* Westport, CT: Praeger, 2005.

Jenny McCarthy   *Louder than Words: A Mother's Journey in Healing Autism*. New York: Dutton, 2007.

Neil Z. Miller   *Vaccines: Are They Really Safe and Effective?*. Santa Fe, NM: New Atlantean Press, 2008.

Martin Myers and   *Do Vaccines Cause That?! A Guide for*
Diego Pineda   *Evaluating Vaccine Safety Concerns*. Galveston, TX: Immunizations for Public Health, 2008.

Paul Offit   *Autism's False Prophets: Bad Science, Risky Medicine, and the Search for a Cure*. New York: Columbia University Press, 2008.

———   *Vaccinated: One Man's Quest to Defeat the World's Deadliest Diseases*. New York: HarperCollins, 2007.

Robert Sears   *The Vaccine Book: Making the Right Decision for Your Child*. New York: Little, Brown, 2007.

Stanley   *The Vaccination Controversy: The*
Williamson   *Rise, Reign, and Fall of Compulsory Vaccination for Smallpox*. Liverpool, UK: Liverpool University Press, 2008.

Periodicals

Jill U. Adams   "Contagious Disease's Spread Highlights Dilemma over Unvaccinated Kids," *Los Angeles Times*, February 23, 2009.

Austin American- Statesman	"Put Autism Scare over Vaccines to Rest," February 17, 2009.
Alicia M. Bell	"Hold the Hype on HPV," *Women's Health Activist*, May–June 2007.
Sandra G. Boodman	"Faith Lets Some Kids Skip Shots," *Washington Post*, June 10, 2008.
Buffalo (NY) News	"Educate, Don't Mandate: Preteen Cancer Vaccinations Should Be Parental Decision," February 19, 2007.
Christian Science Monitor	"Keeping Choice on the Gardasil Vaccine," February 13, 2007.
Cincinnati Post	"A Promising Approach," February 10, 2007.
Marcus A. Cohen	"Prevention of Cancer Associated with Human Papilloma Virus: A New Merck Vaccine vs. Nutritional Approaches," *Townsend Letter: The Examiner of Alternative Medicine*, June 2007.
Rebecca Coombes	"Life-Saving Treatment or Giant Experiment?" *British Medical Journal*, April 7, 2007.
Mark Finch	"Point: Mandatory Influenza Vaccination for All Health Care Workers? Seven Reasons to Say 'No,'" *Clinical Infectious Diseases*, April 15, 2006.

Sigrid Fry-Revere "Be Careful About Hype Before Mandatory HPV Vaccines," *Detroit News*, April 24, 2007.

Renee Gerber "Mandatory Cervical Cancer Vaccinations," *Journal of Law, Medicine, & Ethics*, Fall 2007.

Ellen Goodman "Good Vaccine Gets Bad Push," *Buffalo (NY) News*, March 5, 2007.

Denise Grady "A Vital Discussion, Clouded," *New York Times*, March 6, 2007.

Penny Harrington "Talking Points: The HPV Vaccine," Concerned Women for America, February 12, 2007. www.cwa.org.

Bernadine Healy "Don't Rush to Judgment," *U.S. News & World Report*, February 26, 2007.

Gail H. Javitt, Deena Berkowitz, and Lawrence O. Gostin "Assessing Mandatory HPV Vaccination: Who Should Call the Shots?" *Journal of Law, Medicine, & Ethics*, Summer 2008.

Terence Jeffrey "Socializing Sexual Risk," *Townhall.com*, January 17, 2007. www.townhall.com.

Claudia Kalb "Stomping Through a Medical Minefield," *Newsweek*, October 25, 2008.

Lancet "Should HPV Vaccines Be Mandatory for All Adolescents?" October 7, 2006.

Maura Lerner	"Health Employers Giving Flu Vaccine a Shot in the Arm," *Minneapolis Star Tribune*, September 29, 2008.
Megan McArdle	"The Poking Cure," *Atlantic*, March 28, 2008. www.theatlantic.com.
New York Times	"A Vaccine to Save Women's Lives," February 6, 2007.
Judy Norsigian, Alicia Priest, and Robin Barnett	"Gardasil: What You Need to Know About the HPV Vaccine," *Network*, Spring–Summer 2007.
Kate O'Beirne	"A Mandate in Texas: The Story of a Compulsory Vaccination and What It Means," *National Review*, March 5, 2007. www.nationalreview.com.
Paul A. Offit and Charlotte A. Moser	"The Problem With Dr. Bob's Alternative Vaccine Schedule," *Pediatrics*, January 2009.
Rick Perry	"My Order Protects Life," *USA Today*, February 8, 2007.
Alan G. Phillips	"Refusal to Vaccinate Forms Raise Ethical Questions," *Townsend Letter: The Examiner of Alternative Medicine*, May 2008.
Andre Picard	"Why Politics and Public Health Don't Mix," *Toronto Globe & Mail*, February 21, 2008.
Seattle Times	"A Serious Campaign Against Cervical Cancer: The Newspaper's View," February 21, 2007.

Peter Sprigg   "Pro-family, Pro-vaccine—but Keep It Voluntary," *Washington Post*, July 15, 2006.

USA Today   "Rush to Require Cancer Shot Threatens to Promote Backlash," February 8, 2007.

Lynne K. Varner   "We Can Obsess over S-E-X or Help Save Young Lives," *Seattle Times*, January 31, 2007.

Washington Times   "Inoculating," February 28, 2007.

Elizabeth M.   "Cancer Triumph and Travail,"
Whelan   *Washington Times*, June 15, 2006.

Ram Yogev   "Influenza Vaccine Confusion: A Call for an Alternative Evidence-Based Approach," *Pediatrics*, November 2005.

Index

A

Aborted fetal tissue, 64–67, 68

Adolescent sexuality, 83–84, 89, 90–94

Age (for vaccination)
  autism diagnosis and, 50–51, 52
  early childhood, 16, 45–46
  for Hepatitis B, 35–36
  for HPV, 77–80, 89, 92–93
  See also Children's health

Allen, Arthur, 69–72

Allergic reactions, 15–16, 23, 33, 93

Alternative health care, 29–30

Alternative vaccines, 66

Aluminum, 70–71

Animal cell use, 66

Antibody functioning, 13–14

Arkansas laws, 67

Australia (disease in), 40

Autism possible causes, 51–52

Autism's False Prophets (book), 9

Autism/thimerosal link
  cover-up of studies, 38–39
  lack of connection studies, 50–52
  parental concerns about, 55–56, 59–60
  refutation of studies, 48–50, 70

Autoimmune diseases, 23, 33

B

Bell, Louis M., 42–52

Black, Dr. Dean, 29–30, 31

Blair, Tony, 60

British Medical Journal, 51

C

California laws, 61, 68

Carrey, Jim, 8–9, 71, 72

Catania, David, 83

Catholics, beliefs of, 64, 67

CDC (U.S. Centers for Disease Control and Prevention). *See* U.S. Centers for Disease Control and Prevention

Celebrity vs. science, 71–72

Cervarix, 86–87, 98

Cervical cancer, 77–79, 84–86
  See also HPV vaccine (Gardasil)

Chicken pox vaccine (Varivax), 36, 54, 64–65

Child care laws, 53, 61

Child Protective Services (CPS), 56, 67

Children's health
  adolescent sexuality, 83–84, 89, 90–94
  industry influence over, 35–37
  isolation of the unvaccinated, 58–59, 61–62
  pressure from pediatricians, 36, 54–56
  safety of vaccinations, 17, 44–46, 53–54
  school entry requirements, 39–40, 56, 66–68